GLENN KARWOSKI

CPR

FOR BUSINESS

KEYS TO CREATING POWERFUL REPUTATION

MSP
BOOKS

Minneapolis, MN

For Madelaine
Every day's a holiday with the lemur. . .

220 South Sixth Street, Suite 500
Minneapolis, MN 55402

Copyright ©1999 by Glenn Karwoski

Designed by Jo Davison

Illustrations by Alex Boies

Printed in the United States of America

Library of Congress Catalog Card Number 98-67741

ISBN 0-9641908-0-X

TABLE OF CONTENTS

When *Twin Cities Business Monthly* Editor and Publisher Tom Mason and I sat down and started discussing the possibility of my writing a book, I really had no idea how much work would be involved and how many people and resources I would draw upon to do it. There are many to thank.

The first acknowledgment goes to Tom and MSP Communications for providing the opportunity and for assigning such a great editor to the project in Rebecca Rowland. I must admit, I had mixed emotions when I thought she had slit her wrists after reading the first chapter, only to realize it was red ink. Seriously, her insight and patience for this first-time author were invaluable, and it was fun to work with her. Also at MSP Communications, Brooke Benson was very helpful in managing the production schedule for the project.

I was fortunate to have Jo Davison, the talented creative director at our sister agency, The Edison Group, provide design guidance. And thanks to Jo, I was able to work with a terrific illustrator, Alex Boies.

Having been in the agency business for more than 15 years, I've worked with some outstanding clients and those experiences form the basis for much of the content and thought in this work. I'm grateful for the opportunities. I've also worked with some of the best people in the business, both here at Karwoski & Courage, and throughout our entire parent organization, Martin/Williams. To all of them, I say thanks for making me smarter.

While I've worked on this book for about a year, I'm sure that for some of my friends who have listened to my trials and tribulations, it seems much longer. I thank them all for lending a sympathetic ear and offering encouragement.

When I look back at my career experiences, I owe a debt of gratitude to many, but three people stand apart from the rest. Thanks to Linda Schilling, who gave me my first real break in the business. Thanks to Bob Jones, who was a mentor for years. And last, but certainly not least, thanks to Dave Floren, Chairman of Martin/Williams, who gave me the opportunity to start Karwoski & Courage and is a living example of integrity and reputation to which we can all aspire.

I'm a lucky guy.

by Paul A. Holmes

Editor, *Reputation Management* and *Inside PR* magazines

We are entering an era in which the true value of an organization is best measured not by its balance sheet, but by the strength of the relationships it enjoys with those upon whom it is dependent for its success.

If you want to get a sense of where a company was 12 months ago, or even where it stands today, you can still turn to the annual report. But if you want to predict with any accuracy where a company will be tomorrow, or a year from now, or five years from now, you need to understand the relationships it enjoys with its employees, with its customers, with its shareholders. These are the foundations of success.

An organization that manages those relationships well, that communicates openly, that invests in credibility, that invites and acts on feedback, will respond more appropriately to changes in its operating environment and find all of its constituents more trusting, loyal, more supportive.

Relationships have always been important to organizations, of course, although their value has long been underestimated because it is difficult to measure, and even more difficult to translate into dollars and cents terms. Relationships are becoming more important because we are entering an age of transparency, and era in which absolutely everything an organization does, and even thinks, is destined to find its way into the public realm.

Corporations in the United States operate under more intense scrutiny today than ever before. In addition to the media, regulators and consumer activists and plaintiffs' attorneys are on the lookout for any behavior they deem offensive. The Internet allows even the most isolated critics to broadcast their complaints against a company to the entire world. Companies that fail to respond—and respond credibly—to these critics will find the cost of doing business, from their ability to attract and retain good people to their ability to withstand crisis, increasing significantly.

In this environment, public relations must evolve, and is evolving, from the publicity function that it has been at most organizations to a more sophisticated discipline that is responsible for managing an organization's reputation, the sum of its relationships.

Companies are coming to realize that every action they take has reputational implications, and that these implications need to be considered just as carefully as the operational, financial, and legal implications that have traditionally been the underpinnings of good decision making. This means that the public relations function needs to assume an elevated position within the organization and that the people who manage the function need to rise to the challenge, becoming expert counselors as well as first-rate implementers.

Public relations professionals need to develop the attributes that will make them invaluable in their expanded role. They need to become active listeners, monitoring the external environment and providing a conduit for internal and external audiences to express their views to management. They need to become creative problem solvers, coming up with answers to the questions that keep their CEOs awake at night. They need to become experts on the industries in which they operate, understanding the day-to-day business as well as any line manager. They need to become courageous counselors, unafraid to share information and perspectives that may make them unpopular.

For that reason, this book is particularly timely. Glenn Karwoski is one of a new generation of public relations leaders, individuals within the agency and corporate worlds who have a vision of the future of public relations far broader than its past. That future is one of unprecedented challenge but also of unprecedented opportunity.

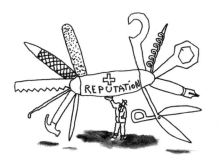

"I cannot hear what you say because what you are thunders so loudly."

Emerson

THE ULTIMATE TOOL

Everyone has it, but do they know how to use it?

Every successful organization has one common element that overshadows all other variables in its importance. It makes no segmentation between large or small organizations, or for profit versus nonprofit. Regardless of industry or domain of expertise, this element transcends balance sheets and mission statements. For those who understand it and make its development the highest of priorities, this element can envelop every aspect of a business and create a golden halo that is almost impossible to dim. For those who ignore it, fail to dedicate the proper resources to its care, or worse, take it for granted as an entitled outcome—this single factor can destroy a business.

What is this seemingly all powerful element? Reputation. **Reputation is your organization's most important asset—or liability. Reputation is a cumulative outcome of the actions of both individuals and the organization.**

It is simultaneously simple and incredibly complex. Yet, if you understand the key ingredients of a powerful, positive reputation and how to strategically and consciously create this kind of reputation for your organization and yourself, you can harness the ultimate tool—one that will impact every part of your organization.

"Reputation—the ultimate tool?" you might ask. Yes, because it is the one element consistent in all organizations that touches and impacts every facet of a business. It is the variable that has the single greatest potential for positive or negative outcome on the greatest number of publics that affect your business—in essence, it is unparalleled in the breadth and depth to which it can influence outcomes. **Of all the variables you can try to control in business, reputation is the single most important one.**

Just how far-reaching can reputation be? Think of all the audiences your organization touches on a daily, weekly, monthly, and annual basis. Multiply that number by the all the contacts those audiences have, and then add the number of individuals this larger group in turn reaches.

Think of how many hundreds of thousands of people shop at a national retailer every day. Now, assume these customers tell one or two people about their shopping experience. The number of individuals exposed to that retailer quickly doubles or triples. As a result, on any given day, a retailer may have several million people experiencing, commenting about, and influencing its reputation—not to mention the millions of people who may see its advertising.

By this simple example, you begin to see how the reach of reputation expands exponentially, well beyond the original environment. Your reputation network extends from consumers who are exposed to your advertising and the customer service people answering a toll-free information line, to the distribution service getting your product to retail shelves and the analysts on Wall Street who track financial performance.

Your reputation has exponential reach and impact.

Another way to examine reputation is through visualizing what its diverse and related components of relationship look like. Reputation is a lot like an international airline with a series of hubs. Each hub represents a different constituency, and the airline transfers passengers and baggage from one location to another. Just like passengers with baggage, reputation is transported, interacting with any number of publics along the way.

The success of the airline comes in part from how its system is managed, but a system of any kind is far from static. A key element of many successful companies is a commitment to not only creating good systems, in this case to meet the needs and goals of both the carrier and the passengers, but also continually refining the system to meet ever changing needs in a dynamic environment. So, just as the airline needs to continually adapt to changing individual and collective needs and environments, organizations must consciously and continually create reputation in an environment filled with diverse passengers and baggage.

And like the airline, when it comes to reputation, you've got to be selective about what kinds of baggage you'll agree to carry and at what cost to the system as a whole.

So, how does an individual or company go about creating reputation?

> *"If I take care of my character, my reputation will take care of itself."*
> **D.L. Moody**

> *"Character is like a tree, and reputation like its shadow. The shadow is what we think of it; the tree is the real thing."*
> **Anonymous**

To the extent that we take action, we create reputation. Using the airline analogy—a carrier could have the most efficient system for managing passenger needs but if the company doesn't create a flight plan and schedule that meets the needs of both the key constituencies and the company, business will undoubtedly suffer. Passengers will go elsewhere. In this respect, reputation is similar; we don't simply manage reputation, we create it.

Southwest Airlines is a great example of a company that works to create reputation by meeting the needs of its key constituents and the needs of the organization itself. By introducing innovative practices that address passenger needs and melding those with operational efficiencies in scheduling and destination cities, Southwest consistently ranks at the top of customer satisfaction lists, as well as at the top of financial performance and employee satisfaction rankings.

Reputation is more than skin deep and it's not something you create once and then continue to manage. It involves multiple, changing factors, so it's never static and therefore requires constant creation and re-creation to meet growing needs and expectations. **Reputation is not a snapshot, it's an endless moving picture with new characters and situations every day.**

It's important to realize the distinction between creating and managing reputation. Recently, the term "reputation management" has gained popularity.

Employing the concept of "reputation management" is acceptable, provided that your definition of management is dynamic and rooted in action. If this is the case, to manage is to take action and in doing so, to create. **Managing reputation is far from preserving the status quo; it's actively understanding what you're after and implementing the strategies and initiatives that help you and your business achieve this goal.**

"In the creative state a man is taken out of himself. He lets down as it were a bucket into his subconscious, and draws up something which is normally beyond his reach. He mixes this thing with his normal experiences and out of the mixture he makes a work of art."

E.M. Forster

Reputation is the result of constant creation. Far from static, the process of generating and managing reputation is constantly evolving. To the extent that to create is to take action, reputation originates both in action and how this action is perceived by others. The perception of action forms the basis of our experience.

"Trust only movement.
Life happens at the level of events,
not of words.
Trust movement."

Alfred Adler

It may be more helpful to think of our experience process as an equation:

ACTION + PERCEPTION OF ACTION = EXPERIENCE

Once we have an experience, we evaluate that experience. It can be positive, negative, or neutral. At that point, we begin to make a judgment about our experience and that forms the foundation of reputation.

EXPERIENCE + EVALUATION = JUDGEMENT AND PERCEIVED REPUTATION

For example, let's say, that you want to use an overnight delivery service to send a package to another state. On the day you send the package, a terrible storm grounds all air traffic in the city from which you're sending the package. The delivery service calls you and explains that your package can't be sent by air and probably won't be delivered until very late the next day. You explain how urgent it is for the package to arrive by the next morning, and the manager of the delivery service then assures you that no matter what, the package will get there on time.

The next day your package not only arrives on time, but you learn the manager of the facility drove his/her own car 400 miles overnight to make sure your package was delivered on time.

What's your opinion of the organization now?

If you plug in the variables of our mini-case study into the equation cited earlier, you can see how reputation begins to take shape. As a result of the company's action (driving all night to deliver your package) you begin to form a perception resulting in your overall experience—great customer service: no matter what, they'll get the job done. Your evaluation of the company's action and your overall experience are the building blocks of this company's reputation. Your experience (very positive) influences your judgment and plays an important role in creating the company's reputation (you feel very positive and will tell others of your experience). Your recommendation of them, though seemingly small at first, is an important factor in their success because you are part of a broader network.

"Motives and purposes are in the brain and heart of man. Consequences are in the world of fact."

Henry Geaye

As individuals, and collectively in organizations, we make conscious decisions about what actions we take. Through the actions we choose to take, we have in our power the ability to create reputation every day.

That's what this book is about—creating reputation. By consciously planning and acting you can ultimately create the reputation you want for your organization and for yourself, and it all begins with understanding and harnessing the ultimate tool.

"There are risks and costs to a program of action. But they are far less than the long-range risks and costs of comfortable inaction."

John F. Kennedy

*"You are here,
and here is wherever I think it is."*

WELCOME TO THE AGE
OF REPUTATION

You are here, and here is wherever I think it is.

Welcome to the age of reputation.

Every major business movement of the past three decades and the advances in technology currently taking place have created the age of reputation. That's what all the discussion about the latest business movement, "branding," is really about. **The era of brand as king is actually the realization on the part of marketers that reputation is important. Building brand is really about building reputation.**

Today, as a culture in the U.S., we exist in a paradoxical situation. We have more information available to us faster than ever before, which enables us to make better decisions, right? Not always. In most instances the amount of information available on any given subject is so overwhelming we don't have time to process it all. This over-abundance of instant information, combined with the technology that makes this data, as well as ourselves, available anywhere at any-time has led to a backlash and a movement toward simplifying. In this scenario, whether you choose to simplify or to keep pace, you don't have time to waste making bad choices. Hence, **brands take on heightened importance, thereby elevating reputation.** In fact, as the discussion of branding evolves, the focus will begin to shift to reputation, because as more sources of information become more affordable to more people, previously unavailable information will be able to be considered in the decision making process—variables that have not been factored in the past because of the difficulty of accessing such information and the cost. This is what is at the core of the emerging knowledge management discipline in business.

How we arrived at the age of reputation can be traced back to the most significant business event of the past few decades—and it's not the advent of the computer or the beginning of the digital age. It's the gasoline shortage of the early 1970s. That's where the seeds of the current age of reputation were planted.

At that time, a shortage of gasoline created major panic among the automobile-dependent United States. Gas prices soared, and at times, fuel was rationed or not available. Almost overnight, American consumers became obsessed with their vehicle's gas mileage.

After years of designing and building large, powerful, gas-guzzling vehicles, a stunned American automobile industry watched as consumers turned to more fuel-efficient automobiles built by the Japanese. Cars that had never been on consideration lists before became preferred. Americans quickly discovered something else about Japanese cars—more than just fuel efficient, the cars were built better than those made in the U.S. and didn't have that guaranteed repeat business factor —"planned obsolescence"—engineered into them.

American automobile manufacturers had assumed that gasoline supplies would be plentiful and they would always dominate domestic sales because people would always want large, powerful vehicles. That's not to say that their entire marketing strategies, which had up to this point been very successful, should have been changed based on a "what if" scenario. However, development of additional branding strategies (flanker brands) could have headed off a disaster (the Japanese provided another marketing lesson when Nissan and Toyota, identifying a growing market for high-performance luxury vehicles developed their Infinity and Lexus brands).

> ### "The secret of business is to know something that nobody else knows."
> **Aristotle Onassis**

Out of this situation, the battleground of quality began to take shape, although it would take a decade before it became clearly identified as such, helped in part by additional factors in the U.S. economy.

In the mid to late 1970s and early 1980s, as the U.S. economy experienced rapid inflation and rising interest rates, value became a consumer buzzword. And when it came to one of the biggest ticket purchases a consumer makes—a vehicle—consumers perceived the American automobile as one of the worst values. As a result, an industry that had once been a proud symbol of freedom, ingenuity, and pride was now a source of embarrassment and confusion. The situation only became worse as U.S. auto makers desperately tried to stem customer defection and rushed poorly designed and engineered vehicles to market to try to compete. The negative experiences consumers had with these Japanese compact "wannabes" succeeded in further damaging an already wounded reputation.

> ### "Everything is worth what the purchaser will pay for it."
> **Publiliud Syrus**

It wouldn't take very long before the U.S. lost ground on another front due to Japan's lower labor costs, higher productivity, and superior product quality—the growing market for consumer electronics. Now, the value beachhead moved through American garages into consumer homes and the "invasion" continued.

The value movement touched other industries inside the U.S. as well, such as retailing where discount stores like Wal-Mart, K-Mart, and Target gained acceptance and made significant inroads against traditional department stores with consumers searching for more value for their dollars and better use of their time with one-stop shopping options.

Don't forget that during this time, the socio-economic phenomena of the "working woman" reached its peak as tens of thousands of women joined the work force in what would mark the most significant change in the American workplace for decades. As dual incomes became the norm and American families began redefining and reassigning roles, time became an increasingly precious commodity.

When American business finally caught its breath and stopped reeling from the gas crisis and inflation, one fact was painfully clear: the quality of American products had declined significantly. And we had lost the most ground to a country that not so long before had a reputation for inferior quality—Japan.

There's nothing like a good crisis to wake people up, but business soon discovered product quality alone was not to be the deciding factor in success. Another reputation variable became apparent that would ultimately lead to the land of brand where we currently reside—and that is service.

Consciously and subconsciously, we look for factors to differentiate products and services. Once quality levels began to improve in the U.S., we began to naturally evolve toward another level of differentiation in the product and service equation—*how* products and services are provided.

Service factors into the overall perceived value of a product and ultimately impacts the reputation formula (Experience + Evaluation = Judgement and Reputation). This becomes more apparent once quality levels become relatively comparable and true product differentiation, outside the realm of marketing communications, becomes more difficult to realize.

Once parity is achieved in one domain, we instinctively search for additional variables to make distinctions that enable us to make decisions. Once performance is comparable between products and satisfies the customer's/client's needs, service becomes an important and powerful distinguishing factor.

Welcome to the world of Tom Peters and the Search for Excellence years.

"It is not the employer who pays wages— He only handles the money. It is the product (and service) that pays wages."

Henry Ford

On the heels of the total-quality-everything decade (mid-1980s through mid-1990s), consultants like Peters pointed out that service was, in fact, part of what determined the overall perception of quality of a product or service. Just because a product or service fulfilled its designated utility to the user, that experience didn't occur in a vacuum. How the product or service was sold, maintained,

. repaired, or replaced also weighed heavily when it came to user value and was a significant determinant as an evaluation variable in the reputation equation.

Two variables—product quality and service—form the core of external product reputation, yet it can be argued that to the end user these are not separate or even dependent variables, but parts of what is one overall element by which a product or service is ultimately labeled and known—its reputation. However, in order to maximize the performance of the whole, the individual components that united form a single entity—in this case reputation—must be examined to determine why something is succeeding or failing. If the process is examined and performance isn't at its peak, change is inevitable.

"There is nothing permanent except change."
Heraclitus

Welcome to reengineering and rightsizing.

The next and most obvious result of the two preceding business movements of quality and service.

After tweaking quality and service standards, someone finally said, "Hey, maybe we should look at how the whole thing is put together and see if there's a better way." That's the crux of reengineering, although countless consultants would like you to believe the premise is more complicated. It's breaking down process to see if it can be done better, faster, for less, and still be rewarding to the people doing the work (although this last component seems to be an afterthought rather than an equally influencing variable in the mix).

Even now, as we begin to evolve from reengineering of process to maximizing the potential of product and service offerings through innovation and creativity in marketing (the branding process), we're firmly in the midst of the age of reputation. While it exists at a more macro-level that transcends product and service branding efforts, reputation is what branding, reengineering, customer service, and quality are all about.

Put all the business movements we've discussed on a continuum, and you'll see a logical evolutionary process that mirrors the product development cycle and touches reputation at every juncture.

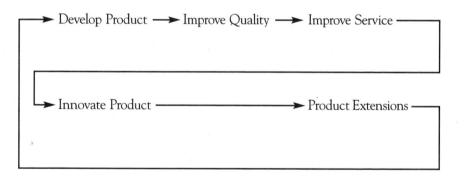

While history allows us to understand and process evolution, information is not necessarily knowledge, so we need to look beyond the basic facts of cyclical business movements to understand the underlying causes that have brought us here, because unless we fully grasp the dynamics of the age of reputation, we run the risk of developing programs that treat obvious symptoms rather than root causes.

So, what's ultimately fueling this age of reputation? We are. Or, to borrow from Pogo, "We've met the enemy, and it is us."

The evolution of business mirrors the evolution of our culture— that's basic marketing. We develop products and services to meet demands, or we create products and services to meet anticipated needs, desires, and demands. **Business has changed radically because our society has changed radically.**

Consider the post-World War II idealized suburban Eisenhower years with *Leave It To Beaver* and *Father Knows Best* role models. They seem like a Norman Rockwell painting compared to the turbulence that followed during the sexual revolution, Vietnam, Watergate, and the gas crisis years. The excessive deal-making designer days of the late 1970s gave way to the recessionary 1980s, and to the present stock market booming, low-interest 1990s.

Back in the 1950s, Ward and June Cleaver weren't divorced, Wally didn't have a chemical dependency problem, and the Beaver didn't go to therapy twice a week to deal with repressed memories of sexual abuse that may or may not be true.
We're in a far different world today. Business as we know it mirrors our world today, and the products and services we've developed are a

reflection of who we are. And who we are today is all about maximizing both our lives and businesses through the speed of information.

"The race is not always to the swift, nor the battle to the strong— but that's the way to bet."

Damon Runyon

Today, technology enables us to work faster, from virtually anywhere on earth, than we could have even just a year ago in our offices. Business is all about speed. Instead of taking days or weeks to process orders, sales data instantly feeds into our automated inventory control systems and products ship overnight. As a result, we have more information available to us today than ever, and it can be delivered to us faster than ever.

A note of caution however: Speed can kill. Just like the deadly pile-ups on the German autobahns, the faster things move, the more serious the collisions when they occur. What does this mean when it comes to reputation? The bad news is that your reputation can be destroyed virtually overnight. Woe is the organization or individual that is slow to respond to reputation allegations. Even *false* reputation allegations can be deadly if an organization or individual is slow to respond. The good news is that it can be redeemed just as quickly—if you know what you're doing.

The key is speed. The trick is harnessing the speed available and using it to your advantage to create, build, and defend the reputation of your brands and of your organization as a whole.

At its core, the current branding machine is being driven by speed, but look beyond branding issues and you'll find a greater factor: reputation. The importance of reputation will only increase in the future. Because our world is moving so fast and we have more demands placed on us than ever before, time is becoming more valuable—time to be with families, time to have more leisure pursuits. And time is only going to become more important as the grim reaper begins to cut a swath through the baby boomer generation, and that tremendously influential segment begins to realize they have less and less of this precious commodity left. So, why does this make brands and ultimately reputation more important for business pursuits? Because people will choose and buy the products and services that allow them to maximize their valuable time. Beyond consumers, the same concept can be applied to employees and other publics.

Companies, people, and products that enjoy more powerfully positive reputations than others will be ones that people choose to associate within their time sensitive environments. People simply won't have time for those with lesser reputations.

"Time gives good advice."

Maltese proverb

It's a one-sided relationship.

UNDERSTANDING REPUTATION

It's a one-sided relationship.

What would someone say if they were asked to describe you? That's reputation, and depending upon who was asked, each answer would probably be different, and reflect that specific individual's experience with you.

While the concept of reputation is easily understood, the process by which it develops is complex. The ultimate outcome of reputation has tremendous implications for individuals and businesses alike.

Take the example of celebrity CEO downsizer, Albert Dunlap. Within months of Dunlap being named CEO of then struggling Sunbeam Corporation, the company's stock price more than doubled. At the time, there wasn't a marked increase in sales or new product announcements. This happened just based on Dunlap's reputation. Of course, when Sunbeam registered disappointing sales and audits revealed some interesting accounting practices, the stock dipped, and the corporate chainsaw cut Al loose with serious impact on the reputations of both Dunlap and the board that hired him in the first place.

This one incident represents a defining reputation moment for Dunlap and for Sunbeam that will follow both for years to come. **Just as Exxon is still haunted by the ghosts of the Valdez oil spill, reputations are powerful, cumulative things that are often times defined and remembered by specific moments in time.**

Even though Exxon has taken great strides to improve its environmental practices following the Valdez spill, its conduct during the spill oftentimes overshadows the otherwise admirable processes the company has put in place since then.

In fact, virtually every business has a reputation that precedes it. Some are based in fact, some in false perception, and some are even based on the spokespeople who represent them. Take a moment to read through the list below, and jot down what images and perceptions come to mind.

NIKE
3M
Ralph Lauren Polo
Ronald McDonald House
Tiffany
Volkswagen

I'll bet you conjured up some powerful images and associated with each image is an opinion or judgment you hold about these companies. For example, your first thought about 3M might have been about one of its popular products like Post-it® Notes or Scotch Brand® tape. Or maybe it was that 3M is an innovative company, which you could have remembered from watching Newton's Apple on PBS, which 3M has sponsored, or from reading one of 3M's advertising messages that focuses on innovation as a core value.

What about NIKE? Did you think, "Just do it," or did you see an image of Michael Jordan floating above the rim ready to slam dunk the company's image into your mind once again. Maybe you thought of former ambassador Andrew Young who was hired by

NIKE to investigate charges of unfair labor practices in third-world countries where its products are manufactured.

The process behind your reputation reasoning for the list of companies just mentioned also applies to people, places, and products. The feelings and attitudes you hold about these things are the result of either the direct or indirect experience you've had with them. That experience, in turn, formed the basis of its reputation, at least as far as you're concerned. If you once took a trip to New York City and had a wonderful time, the city would have more of a positive reputational equity with you than it would for someone whose only experience was reading a negative account of someone else's experience.

If you kept track of all the opinions and judgments you exercise on a daily basis, you would discover the powerful role that reputation plays in your life.

Reputation influences where we live, the products we buy for our home, the food we eat, the transportation we use, the company we work for, and the list goes on and on. That's why there's so much attention being paid to the issue of brand development today. **Powerful brands have powerful reputation. You need strong reputation to have a strong brand. Think about it; ever hear of a strong brand with a weak reputation?**

Because reputation is such an influential factor in the marketing process, the way reputation is created needs to be understood if we wish to harness its awesome power.

When you think of reputation, think of a one-sided relationship, because that's exactly what it's about. The reputation that some person, place, or thing has in our minds is based on our thought process, and while we're influenced by a myriad of factors, the ultimate decision about reputation is ours alone. While we're forming opinions, other people are doing the same in regard to us and the organizations we work for every day as well.

> ### "When we receive "news" from our environment, it is neither good nor bad until our appraisal process has passed judgment."
>
> **Pierce J. Howard, The Owner's Manual For The Brain**

> ### "The environment is everything that isn't me."
>
> **Albert Einstein**

At the root of reputation is appraisal/evaluation/judgment, and it's definitely a head game. That's what Trout and Ries wrote about when they titled their now legendary book about marketing, *Positioning: The Battle for Your Mind.*

Psychologist R.S. Lazarus identifies the relationship of goals to experiences as the key factor in how individuals gauge what their appraisal of an experience will be. **There are three primary questions that we ask in order to make an appraisal of something, and that in turn determines what reputation will be created.**

Making Appraisals

1. Goal relevance: Does this news relate to one of my goals or values?

2. Goal congruence or incongruence: Does this news serve to enhance or thwart my goals or values?

3. Goal content: How is my ego involved? (response to this taps appropriate

emotional response
(anger, joy, guilt, satisfaction, etc.)
from R.S. Lazarus, *Emotion and Adaptation*, 1991.

How these factors are influenced is how reputation is created, so if you want to influence reputation, understand and "control" for these variables.

We selfishly create reputation most of the time. That's not to say that we're always out for ourselves, but the majority of appraisals we make are based on our own agendas. It's what lifestyle marketing and one-to-one marketing is all about. It's why we're bar-coded and scanned and processed into PRIZM® cluster cells (a geo-demographic research tool developed by Claritas Research that utilizes consumer cluster analysis to understand consumer behavior) and VALS™ types (a psychographic research tool developed by the Stanford Research Institute that interprets consumer attitudes and behavior through understanding values and lifestyles). Because the more marketers know about us and can appeal to our goals, the more favorable appraisals we'll make about their products.

Companies that understand how appraisals are created and can relate their products and services to the individual and collective goals people have, will succeed to a far greater extent than the companies that don't. Just remember how the Japanese automobile industry met consumer goals in a way the U.S. companies didn't during the gas crisis and ensuing value-conscious years.

Companies that succeed in winning the appraisal battle in your mind do so quite consciously. They set out from the beginning to establish their reputation. They consciously create.

Wally Olins, a corporate identity expert, asserts that a company can project four things:

1. who it is
2. what it does
3. how it does it
4. where it wants to go in the future.
   (from *Marketing Aesthetics, The Strategic Management of Brands, Identity and Image,* Schmitt & Simonson.)

If you look at the four areas that Olins cites, all of them relate directly to creating reputation. Two of the four areas Olins notes create overall reputation—what a company does and how it does it defines who or what it is.

Olins's last projection for a company—where it wants to go in the future—provides a vision to drive future reputation efforts.

Keep this expanded syllogism in mind:

The manifestation of thought or instinct creates action. Action creates experience. Experience creates the basis for appraisal. Appraisal creates the basis of reputation.

Therefore, action creates reputation.

The application of Olins's corporate identity formula to the expanded syllogism above yields a reputation equation that looks like this:

What we do
+How we do it
Who we are.

What we want to be is calculated:
+ What we choose to do
+ How we choose to do it
Who we will become.

Just like a mathematical equation, the variables we insert change the ultimate outcome. We don't think of ourselves as walking reputation calculators, but that image isn't far from reality. So if you want to take charge and create a powerful reputation, you'll need to start evaluating and programming the variables in your reputation equation.

"Every man is more than just himself; he also represents the unique, the very special and always significant and remarkable point at which the world's phenomena intersect, only once in this way, and never again."

Herman Hesse

In summary, the process looks something like this:

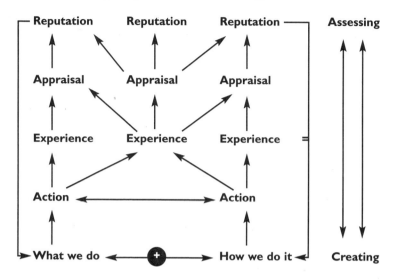

CPR—getting to the heart of the matter.

KEY REPUTATION VARIABLES

My reality of who you are is, until proven otherwise, my truth about your reputation.

In order to consider reputation, you need to examine the reality that others hold about your reputation. In other words, get to know what other people—specifically, key audiences that can make or break your organization—think about you. Now is the time to discover what your reputation really is among the individuals and groups that really count.

Whether you realize it or not, most organizations engage in reputation research on an ongoing basis. Customer satisfaction surveys, toll-free help lines, consumer product focus groups, employee retention rates, and, on the most macro level, overall sales, profit, dividends, and share price, are all reputation barometers. Most of us, however, look at only one or two of these measurable segments at a time.

To determine your organization's overall reputation, you have to look above and across multiple audience segments. Why? Because positive reputation equity translates to bottom-line results in all of your organization's key relationship areas.

From a financial bottom-line, the companies found on *Fortune* magazine's list of most admired companies—a direct reflection of reputational equity—consistently post higher ten-year returns on equity than lesser-rated rivals, according to Professor Charles Fombrun of NYU's Stern School of Management.

And it doesn't end there.

Fombrun goes on to explain that reputation is a powerful variable in the price/value equation. He terms the ultimate sum of the price/reputation relationship reputational capital, and defines the relationship between the two:

"When a company serves its constituents well, its name becomes a valuable asset. It creates reputational capital—a form of intangible wealth that is closely related to what accountants call "goodwill" and marketers term "brand equity." A company with a large stock of reputational capital actually gains competitive advantage against rivals because its reputation enables it to charge premium prices for its products, to achieve lower marketing costs, and to benefit from greater freedom in decision making. In other words, reputation building is a form of "enlightened self-interest."

[from Charles J. Fombrun, *Reputation: Realizing Value from the Corporate Image*, (Boston: Harvard Business School Press, 1996), 11.]

Look no further than the driveways and highways of America to see reputational capital in action: Automobile manufacturers like BMW and Mercedes can charge premium prices for their vehicles because of the reputation capital they've amassed over the years. It's the same reason an engagement ring from Tiffany's has special meaning.

Of course the way these products are made and how they perform are critical variables as well; quality of workmanship and performance are also part of the "how" in our reputation equation.

Despite their importance, however, the areas of profitability, pricing, workmanship, and performance aren't the only places where reputation can generate measurable results. Attracting and retaining a quality personnel base is an arena where reputation reaches into the very heart of your organization, especially in today's tight labor market.

One of the emerging trends in business is the extraordinary mobility and independence of talented professionals and craftspeople. Competition for talent is fierce, and in some cases, organizations aren't just competing against another company for talent. They are facing the growing trend toward self-employment.

For instance, in an ultra-competitive environment, how do you recruit and retain talent? What about if what you're offering, at least on the surface, doesn't seem very desirable at all? Imagine an opportunity to work for an established mega-corporation where you'll be one of thousands of employees enjoying a geographic climate that features six months of winter where sub-zero temperatures are the norm. Sound daunting? If you're Minnesota-based 3M—no problem.

While Minnesota may boast a high quality of life, after you've spent a few winters in the Upper-Midwest, you know that people don't come to work for 3M because of the weather. Top scientists come to the St. Paul campus of 3M because of a different type of climate that is conducive to innovative work. 3M provides its research and development people dedicated lab time during the work week to focus on their own projects. This commitment is part of a total organizational goal of creating a culture of innovation.

"At 3M, managers are an integral part of that innovative company's creative energy. They regularly organize internal trade shows that let different departments share one another's brainstorms and inspirations. The result of the cross-pollination of ideas is a perpetual state of challenge—a vigorous spirit of creative competition. It was in 3M's culture of challenge that Art Fry invented Post-its. Today, to stimulate continuous innovation, 3M aims to have young products—no more than five years old—earn at least 25 percent of its annual profits."

[from John Kao, *Jamming: The Art and Discipline of Business Creativity*, (New York: HarperCollins), 99.]

Reputation assessment doesn't end there. It extends beyond the boundaries of profit and loss and employee recruitment and retention to another key area, one that exerts a powerful influence on the two variables previously mentioned. This critical factor is "word on the street"—what is reported about you, your products, and your company that in turn reaches not only end-users but current and prospective employees.

> *"Today's reporter is forced to become an educator more concerned with explaining the news than with being first on the scene."*
>
> **Fred Friendley**

Media relations—how your organization is portrayed in industry and general business and consumer media—is a very important tool and powerfully influences your reputation. Are you portrayed as a leader, innovator, good corporate citizen? Or has your CEO been blasted by the business media and your product recalled? Are there protesters lined outside your headquarters, or are the community newspapers filled with letters to the editor thanking you for a year's worth of support for local causes.

Like it or not, the media exerts a powerful influence over your reputation, and both the actions you take (or fail to take) and how they are reported can be the difference between key audi-

ence kudos or condemnation. Some of the best examples can be found in the realm of crisis communications, or how an organization responds when it is under fire. One of the classic examples is the Exxon Valdez:

> "There was a window of opportunity with the news media. The reporting initially and for a period of time following the disaster was factual and pretty straightforward even though media representatives were undoubtedly as horrified as the rest of us at the scope of the disaster. But as Exxon stumbled, fumbled, stonewalled, denied, shifted the blame, ducked responsibility and tried to manage the messages, the news media had no choice but to turn against them as well."

> [from James E. Lukaszewski, "Managing bad news in America: It's getting tougher and it's getting worse," *Vital Speeches of the Day* 56/18 (1990), p. 572—from Lawrence Susskind and Patrick Field, *Dealing with an Angry Public: The Mutual Gains Approach to Resolving Disputes,* (New York: The Free Press, a division of Simon & Schuster, 1996), 199.]

These three key variables in assessing reputation—end users, employees, and the media—will be our focus as we examine how to create powerful reputation.

To gain perspective, the first thing you will need to do is review your organizational standing with end users, employees, and the media. With this knowledge in hand, you will have a solid understanding of where your current reputation stands, and this will enable you to identify your reputational strengths and weaknesses and guide you as you move forward.

The map is not the territory.

EVALUATING THE VARIABLES

You are here, and here is wherever I think it is.

When it comes to creating your reputation, the map is not the territory. In fact, it's not even close. The truth in the matter is: THE MAP doesn't exist. The reason the map doesn't exist is because in a world of speed and expanding communication you deal with millions of overlapping territories that change on a daily basis.

Consider the numerous and diverse publics you and your organization have contact with on a daily, weekly, monthly, quarterly, and annual basis. Then, multiply that figure by the number of individuals and companies your contact touches within a particular group. You quickly begin to see why it's impossible to draw a map. You'd need thousands, if not millions of maps to plot all of the territories you and your reputation visit.

But you need to start somewhere, so try this.

Everyone has a map of you. Everyone has a map of your company. And when it comes to you and your company, what they think the territory is—IS your territory as far as they're concerned.

To put it another way:

You are what I think and say you are. Whatever my experience with your product, good or bad, is what I will be inclined to share with others. How do you get a handle on this? How do you get your reputation bearings? And if everyone can map you and your organization, why can't you? Well, you can, to some extent, provided that you understand that what you're developing is not so much a map as it is a guide that can provide a general sense of being and direction. Don't be fooled, though. This guide is not precise, and it's subject to change—daily. How's that for daunting?

That's the nature of reputation territory.

While it may seem like an overwhelming task to get a handle on your reputation, it's not impossible if you view the process as an ongoing exercise of surveying the general category of territories and revising your guide (not map) on a regular basis. Just like radar continually sweeps the skies for signs and locations of activity, your radar must sweep for reputation because it's a moving target.

It may be most helpful to think back to the airline analogy in Chapter One as applied to reputation. **You and your organization are the pilots of the carriers that transport the multiple publics that hold opinions about your reputation. These publics bring baggage that holds the cumulative experiences and events they've had and now helps them form their opinions regarding your reputation. These publics carry this baggage (opinions) wherever they go. And where are these publics going? Their destination is where your "flight" of actions take them. Your actions are continually moving publics from one location to another on a never-ending reputation journey.**

Are your flights on time? Do you know where you're going? If you do not have a clear destination—reputation purpose—in mind, then your actions will not be optimally coordinated to best create and nurture your reputation. In this respect, make certain you have clear reputation goals—destinations—and that they're grounded in reality. Fantasy Island does not exist.

Psychologist Karen Horney has a concept she calls "the idealized self", traces of which can be found to lesser or greater extent in virtually every organization. The premise of the concept is that we all have an idealized vision of who we are, and that vision is usually better in some, or all, ways in comparison to the reality of who we really are. If nothing else, it's at least different from how others perceive us. On a personal level, it may be the out-of-shape, overweight, fifty-year-old that still looks in the mirror and sees a young, trim, athlete. In an organization, it could be the high-turnover sweat shop that still sees itself as a great place to work or a company that hasn't had a product of any significance in years, yet insists on calling itself a leader and innovator.

> *"We judge ourselves by our motives and others by their actions."*
> **Dwight Morrow**

As a result of what is perceived as the idealized organization, CEOs and others often cross the line between being aspirational and being delusional. It's one thing to aspire and proclaim what you want to be. However, to assert you're something that you're not is nothing short of delusional.

Getting in touch with your reputation by honestly evaluating the variables involved helps you to avoid being or becoming a self-idealized organization. It ensures that the guide you're developing is for territory that really exists, rather than being a figment of some CEO's wishful imagination or yours.

To avoid the trap of the idealized organization and gain a firm grasp of reality—understanding who your organization is, what it is really about, and the different perceptions key publics hold about it—you need to be concerned about two basic areas—internal and external audience perception. On the surface, it seems simple, but it's not easy. Not easy when you go beyond these broad distinctions and begin to examine the finer points or subsets of these two categories. How does your organization rank in the areas of employee benefit programs for single mothers? This is just one subset of internal perceptions. Where do you stand in the realm of broadcast advertising? This is an example of an area that affects external perception. You'll need to establish some benchmark or approximate setting among the key groups in these two categories in order to determine where you're starting from on your truth-seeking reputation journey.

When thinking of the process as a journey, consider the airline hub analogy again. When planning a trip you have to know not only your destination but your starting point. A trip to New York City from northern New Jersey requires far different planning than a journey to New York City beginning in Fargo, North Dakota. The same thing holds true when it comes to the reputation journey. You may know where you want to go, or what you'd like your reputation to be, but you're going to have a hell of a time getting there if you don't know the place from which you're starting.

So, in planning the journey, you need to understand the perceptions of key publics and subsets of internal and external audiences. All of these groups accompany us, like them or not. Who are the subsets of internal and external audience perceptions? I'll begin with internal audiences, because they are the most important.

"One doesn't discover new lands without consenting to lose sight of the shore for a very long time."

Andre Gide

INTERNAL AUDIENCES

The employees, partners, and members of an organization are the people who establish the vision, set the goals, create the products, and provide the services. They are the organization, and their cumulative effort creates the organization's overall reputation.

By understanding some of the basic influencers in this group, you'll be able to gauge where the internal temperature of the organization falls. Short of initiating a complete internal policy and communication audit—which you may want to consider at some point, if you haven't done so already—analyzing some key areas can provide a gauge of internal perceptions of reputation.

Areas you should look at include personnel policies and benefits, communications, industry standing, and community standing.

PERSONNEL POLICIES AND BENEFITS

• How does your organization compare to your competitors, as well as to organizations outside of your domain whose reputation you admire? If you want to attract talent from other organizations and disciplines, this is a key area. In addition to traditional comparison areas like health care, insurance, and retirement programs, look at how innovative you are when it comes to gain-sharing, flextime, and other non-traditional policies and programs. Do you have progressive policies for family leave and funding continuing education?

• Imagine that you weren't currently working at your organization—is it the type of place that would appeal to you?

• What type of environment do you create for employees? Is it high energy with creative spaces; a place where freedom of expression is encouraged and opinions equally valued? While you can't definitively place a bottom-line dollar value on environment's impact on psyche, it's becoming more important. Some organizations and employees regard creative work environments as a "perk."

COMMUNICATIONS

Although personnel policies and benefits "communicate" to employees, more formal written, visual, and electronic communication of organizational information is essential to educate and inform employees about developments that may have individual and organizational impact.

• How honest are you in dealing with your employees? For instance, do you keep them informed in a timely manner, or do they have to read the newspaper to find out what's going on in the organization?

• How do you communicate with people, and how do you foster communication among people? Remember, how you communicate something can be as important as the content of the message itself. Take a look at the companies you admire—what are they doing and how does it compare to your organization?

INDUSTRY STANDING

• What does your trade group say about you? Are you a leader? What comments do peers make about your organization? Employees want to take pride in the organization for which they work. Your standing within your industry group is a driving force in how employees will view the organization. Remember, we tend to base our judgements and evaluations on comparison.

COMMUNITY STANDING

• What standing does your organization have in the community? Keep in mind that the members of your organization are also members of the community. What friends and neighbors think and say about an organization can be a source of tremendous pride or embarrassment.

- Depending on the type of organization and industry you're in, you may have other internal subsets. To borrow a point from twelve-step programs, you need to take a "fearless" inventory in order to determine the starting point of your internal reputation journey.

EXTERNAL AUDIENCES

External factors are those outside the boundaries of the organization's walls. They're the subsets that apply the multiplying factor in the reputation equation, and while many sets can exist, some weigh more heavily than others. Let's take a look at four major external influencer groups or areas—suppliers, production and regulators, customers, and the media.

Suppliers

The people who supply the materials that enable you to build the product are critical. Without the raw materials needed to build your product, you have no product. How's that for a blinding flash of the obvious? Although it's a simple fact, it's not necessarily easy to understand the breadth and depth of the supply chain.

This group extends beyond the individuals that take your orders. These relationships can extend to labor unions and beyond national boundaries to foreign countries, involving trade negotiations related to national policy issues that dictate pricing and import quotas (and you thought you were just ordering some metal clips). **All one has to do is to look at recent labor and trade policy history for a powerful reminder that the suppliers of materials you need to create your products are a very key influencer group.** And that includes the transportation suppliers that deliver those materials to you.

When was the last time you recognized your key suppliers? What do they think of your organization. Ever think of asking them how you could improve the production or delivery of your products? Remember, without these people, your ability to create more of your current products, develop new products, and distribute both current and new products is severely limited.

PRODUCTION AND REGULATORS

People who regulate your ability to produce and market your product are equally critical. In our economic system, we often take for granted our ability to develop and sell products. However, regulation is very real and worth exploring if you plan to grow your business. Remember when there was just one huge phone company? Still have doubts about the impact that government regulation can have? Look at the airline industry.

Businesses shouldn't just be concerned about monopoly and anti-trust issues. **Environmental regulations, trade policies and other regulatory programs form a complex and often confusing maze that businesses navigate.** The impact can be tremendous. And don't forget why millions of dollars are spent every year on lobbyists at state and federal levels, not to mention trade associations and quasi-proprietary think tanks. Add to that list an ever-growing number of special interest groups with their own agendas, and you begin to see why you should be very concerned about where your reputation stands with this segment of key influencers.

Issues that have far-reaching consequences for business appear every day. From trade quotas, to minimum wage requirements, to the American Disabilities Act—the ability to run your business is impacted by regulators, probably more than you're aware. Creating a powerful reputation with legislators, trade associations, community leaders, and special interest groups will directly and indirectly impact your ability to influence the environment in which your business operates.

> *"It is useless for the sheep to pass resolutions in favour of vegetarianism while the wolf remains of a different opinion."*
> **Dean William R. Inge**

CUSTOMERS

Don't forget about the people buying your product.

> *"A person buying ordinary products in a supermarket is in touch with his deepest emotions."*
> **John Kenneth Galbraith**

This is the group that most businesses focus on when it comes to their reputation efforts. These are the consumers of your products and services and without them you would have no market for what you produce and sell. No market, no sales, no business.

People choose to buy based on needs and wants, either real or perceived, and when they buy, it's usually based on reputation. Even when a purchase is principally price-driven, reputation is still a primary consideration.
No one consciously buys a product with a poor reputation—tell me, how many Yugos do you see on the road today?

Consumers may be moved to trial purchase and usage by image, but the reputation created by the experience of trial and subsequent usage is eventually evaluated and reported. Then reputation determines the long-term viability of the product. Usually, the more "considered" the purchase, the more reputation will be a factor. "With products that are more costly, complicated, and subtly differentiated, the customer has more at stake. For example, when shopping for a car, the customer will consider price, quality, maintenance costs, resale value, design, safety, subjective appeal—all the aspects that make people pore over Consumer Reports and car magazines. (from Regis McKenna, *Real Time*.)

THE MEDIA

You also must be mindful of people who evaluate the performance of your product, or comment about your product and company, and have an extensive distribution source for their evaluations.

This group is primarily made up of the writers, reporters, critics, and reviewers that have access to millions of consumers through the media. But even this group is growing to include consumers that have access to the Internet where experiences and opinions about your company can be posted and transmitted to millions of people around the world in seconds.

As referenced in the previous section on people who make purchase decisions by consulting sources like Consumer Reports, Regis McKenna asserts that the psychological and financial risks of making a purchase can be reduced by references (appraisals). **Because of widespread and segment-specific distribution, the media are a primary source for people to turn to in order to find perfor-**

mance evaluations—where to go to eliminate the stress of making a bad purchase decision.

The impact of these large information distributors goes beyond the media and can include services like credit bureaus and bond rating services. However, we'll limit our discussion to the most ubiquitous and powerful of information distributors, which are the media. The reason the media are the most powerful is because they are perceived to be the most objective of all information sources. They have more credibility than anything other than personal experience, because a reported account or evaluation that is transmitted through the media is based on someone's personal experience.

Information distribution, when applied to media is known as media relations. Using IBM as an example, Northwestern University Professor Thomas Harris says:

"IBM believes that media relations plays an integral role in market-driven corporate communications programs and holds an important edge over every other tool of communications because of its high credibility. Media relations is one of the "balanced set of communications tools" used by the company to drive target audiences through the "purchase path" from 1) awareness to (2) interest to (3) desire to (4) action. Other tools include advertising, business shows, fields network television, sales promotion, publications, and direct response advertising.

"In its communications to marketing managers, IBM explains that the general public, despite some cynicism about advertising, continues to believe what is seen in the local and trade papers and broadcast on the evening news. Publicity has the impact of a respected third-party endorsement.

When IBM activity is in the news, the report can generate far more word-of-mouth publicity than any advertisement." (from Thomas L. Harris, *The Marketer's Guide To Public Relations*.)

What is reported about your business has a powerful impact on its reputation—the greater the credibility of the media source and its distribution, the greater the impact. And remember, the Internet is a medium that should not be overlooked or ignored. A university professor in Virginia noticed a flaw in the Intel Pentium processor, and after his "discussion" about it on the Internet, the topic became not only a worldwide media story overnight but also the subject of media analysis about the potential impact the discovery would have on the company.

INVESTORS

"You build on cost and you borrow on value."
Paul Reichmann

Another key external group is the one made up of people who finance your organization. While you could argue that the financial community that funds business—through loans, stock offerings, and other transactions—is included in all of the other categories, the money people bear special consideration. For publicly traded companies, there are rules that regulate how and when information about the company can be disseminated. Investor relations is a specialized area of information distribution that communicates financial news about a business to the people and institutions that have invested in the business.

Billions of dollars are gained and lost on a daily basis via stock exchanges, boards of trade, and other related entities throughout the world. Millions of people have savings, investment, and retirement moneys in financial instruments like common stock, mutual funds, government bonds, and certificates of deposit. And the reason behind the investment is not always performance, as some people would assume, but reputation. Millions of dollars are invested daily based on reputation, sometimes unwisely.

Can you remember ever going to the store and buying a Berkshire-Hathaway? When people invest in Berkshire-Hathaway, they're really investing in the reputation of Warren Buffet and his ability to make sound and very successful financial decisions.

Another reason to create powerful reputation with investors is because the relationship of a business with the financial community is often reported to all of the other groups via the media.

It's all up to you.

WHERE DO WE GO FROM HERE?

"My interest is in the future because I am going to spend the rest of my life there."

—Charles F. Kettering

Where you go from here depends on what you choose to do and how you do it. Looking back to the Olins formula of corporate identity, the reputational equation looks like this:

What we do
+How we do it
Who we are

Moving into the future, the variables we plug into the equation below will determine what our reputation becomes:

What we choose to do
+How we choose to do it
Who we will become

By applying the equation above to all of the sub-segments of audiences covered in the last chapter, you will create your overall reputation. For example, look at Barney's, the now tony retailer that started out as a discount men's clothing store with one location on Seventh Avenue in New York City. Today, Barney's is known for incomparable style not only in men's clothing but also women's apparel and home furnishings. Its Madison Avenue store in

Manhattan has a well-regarded restaurant, and it recently opened a health club that offered membership by invitation only.

Barney's went from discounter to style arbiter. How did Barney's do it? By establishing a vision of what it wanted to become and then having that vision guide its actions. Knowing that its goal was to become one of, if not the, premier fashion retailers in the country, the merchandise mix changed. Store personnel changed. The way the stores looked changed. Advertising and promotion changed. In essence, Barney's changed everything about what it did and the manner in how it was done. In doing so, Barney's realized its vision of who it wanted to be.

Just as management guru Stephen Covey urges, begin with the end in mind when creating who you want to become. Then, the variables you choose to execute and how you choose to execute them will flow naturally from the desired end result.

One company that has created reputation from an overall vision and serves as a great example of how to begin with the end in mind is 3M. 3M is all about innovation. In fact, 3M is so innovative it's taken two basic competencies—abrasives and adhesives—and created hundreds of products in virtually every business and consumer category. But the 3M story is not just one of top-notch, cutting-edge development; it's about a total commitment to a vision of innovation that has produced one of the most powerful reputations in business today.

3M fosters a culture of innovation by allowing its scientists time to work on projects of personal interest to them. So, in addition to an employee's regular salary and benefits, 3M gives its research and development people something that's in short supply but highly valued—time.

How many companies can you think of that allow employees to

work on projects of personal interest to them on company time? How many of those actually encourage employees to do so?

Yet, that's just one example of 3M's internal innovation. Here's another from personal experience. My agency works with 3M, so I had the opportunity to see first hand how the 3M culture works to foster innovation and team building.

On one project, my team and the marketing people from the 3M division we were working with at the time made a trip to visit a potential event-marketing partner. The 3M team wasn't limited to the marketing staff; another 3M employee, an engineer from the division joined us.

At first I thought it rather odd to have a non-marketing person along for our presentation, since the engineer had no direct role in the project. What was his role in this? Why was he along for the meeting? When I asked, I learned he was attending to observe and to learn more about the role of marketing in the division. Far from unusual, this was actually a regular practice. By observing the marketing people in action and hearing first hand the questions and areas of interest the potential tie-in partner addressed, there's the potential for fresh ideas or at least a greater understanding of roles within the division.

Who knows? The seed of another Post-it brand might have been planted on that date.

These examples of 3M's inner workings provide some insight into how the company chooses to be innovative and how it supports that effort internally.

The same effort is applied externally as well. 3M also enjoys a reputation for innovation that is the direct result and end-product of its internal culture.

Think for a second, could you imagine a work environment without Post-It Notes or Scotch brand tape? These two products and countless others spring from one of 3M's core competencies in adhesive technology. So does its new line of category leading Nexcare waterproof bandages.

3M is always pushing forward, always innovating. Many people have the misguided notion that the only way to innovate is to create new technologies, but that's just the most obvious way. A far more difficult but no less rewarding way for an organization to open or create new markets is by developing new applications and creating new variations of existing technologies.

Look beyond the 3M campus in St. Paul, Minnesota, toward the West Coast and you'll see scores of companies in Silicon Valley literally trying to make their existing products obsolete through innovation. In that environment, reputations change every day, and today's hot new computer technology can be next week's has-been profile. But given the nature of the computer industry and the environment in which companies compete, this is a risk organizations have to be willing to take.

The actions a company chooses to take, as well as the style in which it undertakes those actions, plays a critical role in determining its reputation. Remember that radical start-up called Microsoft? This is a prime example of how quickly reputation can change. Here's an organization that's gone from being an irreverent, hot start-up that changed the way we all do business to a mega-corporate entity that now epitomizes "the establishment" in the software industry.

Don't get me wrong, I'd love to have the reputational equity that Microsoft enjoys. Part of it is an inevitable result of growth, but as the company continues to attract its share of the industry's best and brightest, its increasingly monopolistic and monolithic image (currently 22,000 employees with market value of $270 billion—based on its most recent annual report) is changing the organization's reputation among many publics, most recently capturing the attention of government regulators.

Where you go with your reputation depends on how you evaluate and cultivate the relationships you have with each subsegment of internal and external audiences. In the next chapters, we'll look at examples of how some companies have successfully developed strong reputations with powerful segments of these audiences.

"If you want to be loved, be lovable."
Ovid

Creating Powerful Reputation with external audiences.

THE WORLD AT LARGE

Creating Powerful Reputation with external audiences.

Saturn's reputation among consumers is out of this world, and Target Stores hits the bull's eye every time when it comes to creating a positive reputation. These two are great examples of companies with excellent external reputations, and are worth examining to learn some of their keys to creating the types of reputations others envy. First of all, start by taking a closer look at the simple reputation equation mentioned earlier:

What you do + How you do it = What people think of you (reputation).

When it comes to your overall reputation, you can break down the two added reputation equation variables (what + how) even further. **What you do is another way of saying, "Here's my core competency," but it should extend beyond that and take on an aspirational quality. Your statement of what you do melds purpose and mission, taking into account all your key publics.** Think of writing the first paragraph of a letter that introduces your business to a variety of audiences and you'll begin to get the feeling and tone for defining "what you do."

How you do it defines style and personality. In regard to reputation, if your core competency is as good or better than that of your competitors, this second variable, **"how you do it," is the more powerful and influential variable in determining reputation.**

Although we'll take an in-depth look at two companies that provide insight into these reputation variables, try identifying some distinctions on your own first. The companies listed below are all in similar industries and categories of competition. See if you can identify the distinctions in how they do what they do and the reputation it forms in your mind.

Company	What They Do	How They Do It	Reputation
Cadillac	Luxury Cars		
Lexus	Luxury Cars		
NIKE	Sport gear		
Adidas	Sport gear		
IBM	Computers		
Apple	Computers		
New York Times	News		
USA Today	News		
Oprah	Talk Show		
Jerry Springer	Talk Show		
Disneyworld	Vacations		
Club Med	Vacations		

You probably noticed some very distinct differences in the style of how these companies do what they do. The next two companies are reputation leaders in their industries. By closer examination, they provide blueprints for how to shape a distinctive reputation for your organization.

REDEFINING THE CATEGORY: SATURN AUTOMOBILES

Saturn is the relatively new brand launched by General Motors several years ago that revolutionized the automotive industry.

While the automobiles that they build are good, Saturn's "what we do" is not it's distinguishing reputation variable. In terms of performance and appearance, the cars are nothing special. In terms of competence and quality they're near or equal to most competitors, and in some cases better. Saturn's "how we do it" is really what distinguishes them from the competition and has created a very strong, differentiated brand.

Creating internal reputation is addressed in the following chapter, but I'll reference what Saturn has done in that arena now because these internal workings drive so much of their external marketing and reputation building (as is often the case in successful companies). **In fact, what Saturn does internally results in its most powerful external marketing communications tool.**

From the outset, Saturn was going to do things differently, and it started at the very foundation of its business by re-tooling the traditional approach to dealing with labor unions and contracts. Saturn has a different kind of "contract" with its employees, one that is unlike any other in the automobile industry. In fact, Saturn's contract with the United Auto Workers (UAW) Union is different from that of the rest of its General Motors (GM) counterparts.

One of the distinguishing factors of the contract is Saturn

employees have a special profit-sharing incentive other GM divisions do not. Therefore, they have more at stake when they build a car. **Cleverly illustrating its "employee-owners" as part of its overall brand advertising message, Saturn translates this and other internal policies into external marketing strategies and reputation creation.**

Saturn's distinguishing qualities don't stop there. Another facet of Saturn's business—its dealer network—has been a key ingredient in creating a powerful reputation for the company and another factor that has translated into positive reputation equity. While some studies say that people actually enjoy haggling over prices with car salespeople, the majority don't relish the experience and actually regard it as one of the more unpleasant transactional tasks in life. Taking a different approach, Saturn decided to eliminate the negotiating of price, perceived by most people as a negative part of the car buying experience. Instead, it offered its best deal on the sticker price. This innovation revolutionized the car buying experience and was just another way Saturn separated itself from competitors.

So, not only do the people that build Saturn automobiles approach their task differently, but the way the car is marketed to the general public is different as well. This is not your typical car company.

By creating a no-haggle sales environment, Saturn's sales people are able to focus on the features, advantages, and benefits of owning a Saturn automobile and function more as consultants than the stereotypical slick, high-pressure, let's-make-a-deal types. Satisfaction surveys show that Saturn customers appreciate the process, and the quality of sales employees the company attracts are of a higher caliber than that of its competitors. A well publicized example was that of a recently graduated Ivy Leaguer being so impressed with the Saturn sales process, he applied for a job and became a Saturn "consultant." The company's advertising regularly points out the helpful qualities of its sales consultants with real life case histories such as one consultant with a pilot's license flying to pick up a prospective customer from a far-away town (who did indeed buy a car). Can you think of any other automobile manufacturer that highlights its sales personnel in its advertising? It doesn't stop there.

Once you buy a Saturn, you can bring it back for free car washes for as long as you own the vehicle. There are special "get to know your vehicle" service clinics, some with special added touches like barbecues. There has even been a Saturn owners' reunion at the plant in Spring Hill, Tennessee, where customers get to meet the people that built their cars. The reunion brings the process full circle and creates a connection that has never existed in U.S. automotive history. It also serves to forge a stronger bond between owners and the company while elevating the status of the Saturn employees.

What Saturn has done is to form an almost "cult-like" following among its owners. Apart from high-performance U.S. and foreign automobile clubs, there's never been an owners organization group for a "regular" American brand.

Saturn's reputation speaks for itself—as it should. It's a completely different car company—especially in the U.S.—in many employee and consumer-friendly, positive ways. This image runs counter to the negative perception that America had of U.S. auto manufacturers following the gas crisis of the 1970s. Saturn put its money and resources where its mouth is—they don't just claim to be different; they are. **In the reputation formula, Saturn's distinc-**

tiveness is in "how" it does what it does.

By creating layer upon layer of integrated distinctions, Saturn has forged a unique reputation among many publics. And that reputation has been created and supported world-wide through literally millions of dollars worth of media exposure through editorial coverage.

Not only does Saturn utilize paid media to advertise its employee programs and owner reunions, it generates even more exposure through media coverage of its unique internal and external culture. And because third-party coverage is viewed as a form of endorsement by consumers, editorial exposure validates and adds credibility to what the company does.

Whether you choose to buy a Saturn or not, there's no doubt you're aware it's an automobile brand that is differentiated in many positive ways. That's a good reputation to have.

Targeting Powerful External Reputation by Creating a Category

Like its increasingly ubiquitous logo, Target Stores, the largest operating division of Dayton-Hudson Corporation, is a company that hits the bull's eye of creating powerful external reputation.

Target invented and defined the term "upscale discount" store at a time when most people would think the term was an oxymoron. **In reality, Target created a new category of retailing by demonstrating that upscale style and discount prices can be compatible.**

When Target opened its first store in Roseville, Minnesota, in the 1960s, it took what had been a dirty business and cleaned it up—literally. Target Stores were polished, well-organized, and brightly lit. Compared to the shabby, storage bin merchandise discount stores of the day, a neglected segment of the retail industry, Target was a breath of fresh air. Until Target entered the category, discount retailing was a home for discarded, discontinued, and damaged merchandise, and because consumers were getting "deals" they didn't expect much of a shopping experience.

Helped in part by the value movement of the 1970s, which was provoked by the gas crisis and high inflation, Target grew geographically by acquiring poorly run discount chains and following suburban expansion. It began to increase its merchandising and marketing sophistication as well, and today the chain is one of the most admired, and by some accounts, the best in the industry.

Going back to the "what we do" part of the reputation equation (what we do + how we do it = who we are), Target is a retailer that sells name brand and proprietary, "trend-right," quality products at great prices. It's not unusual today to find Target merchandise in upscale home furnishing and fashion magazines—this represents the company's evolution as a trend leader in its category. These roots took hold early in Target's history when the company rocked the industry by selling then trendy Gloria Vanderbilt and Calvin Klein jeans at discounted prices.

Merchandising in and of itself has been a distinguishing characteristic from the beginning, but that wasn't all. As other retailers began to copy Target's successful formula, the "how we do it" part of the formula became more important, and today this is what sets the organization apart from others. **Target's style, its personality, is unique in a powerfully positive way.**

The Target experience is a positive one for consumers on all fronts— in every aspect of reputation.

Let's begin with the now-famous Target Sunday circular. It advertises merchandise in a clean, stylized way. Decades ago, when Target began this weekly advertising vehicle, the concept of a full-color weekly circular for a discount store had never been done before. This was true, at least until other stores found out it was one of the best read "sections" of the Sunday paper for many consumers. Keeping pace with the times, Target is continually updating the well-read circular's look.

Shopping at Target is a pleasant experience that mirrors the image established by not only its weekly supplement but also other advertising and promotional vehicles. Early in its history, Target's clean and well-organized approach to store layouts was one of the most distinguishing and motivating factors for consumers. Rather than resting on its laurels, Target continued to improve its stores and its reputation through ongoing innovation.

In the 1980s, Target's advertising, promotion, and public relations began to evolve. The company started utilizing what has become a steady stream of celebrities in its advertising, PR, and in-store merchandising. In fact, Target's work with music personalities like Amy Grant has created some of the most mutually beneficial marketing programs in the retail and music industries. By working with a cadre of celebrities and sharing reputation equity, Target's promotions continually have "star" quality.

While Target's celebrity promotional programs are powerful, its community relations programs are equally strong and pack a potent external marketing punch. Target, and its parent corporation Dayton-Hudson, is one of the most generous companies in the U.S., donating a fixed percentage of its profits to the communities in which it operates stores. From funding environmental programs for youth to having Robert Redford appear in a Target commercial on behalf of the National Parks System, Target has integrated cause marketing and community relations into its external communications mix with outstanding reputation results. Whether it's helping to restore the Washington Monument or helping kids take part in saving the environment, Target has become the standard by which all other retail cause marketing is measured. And just recently the chain launched a program called "Taking Charge of Education," which donates a percentage of purchases made on a Target charge card directly to local schools designated by customers. Early results, as evidenced by a 1998 new product marketing award from the American Marketing Association, indicate the program is very well received. **When you shop at Target, you're not just buying fashionable merchandise at a good price, you're supporting your local schools and community programs, as well as more broad national initiatives.** How's that for creating reputation. . . and it still doesn't stop.

Target is increasingly expanding its already positive reputation as a style and trend leader. Its merchandise is appearing with more frequency in national style magazines and it even hosts an annual fashion show in New York City.

Beyond the inviting, easy-to-navigate atmosphere inside, there's another level of innovation assisting customers once occupied only by department stores. Target created a bridal registry program just like its more upscale retail sibling that allows couples-to-be to roam through a store and scan all the merchandise they'll need for their new life together. The program not only strengthens the bond that the couple already has with Target by making the store part of one of the most significant events in their lives, it also offers wedding guests the opportunity to purchase reasonably priced gifts. And if one of the guests is not familiar with Target, the registry program doubles as an introduction to the store. Lullaby Club® is the same premise adapted for parents-to-be, again making Target part of peoples' lives through a connection that could be viewed as the ultimate in event marketing—developing a relationship with consumers and their extended families and friends by being part of the most personal and meaningful events in their lives.

Developing programs like these, Target forges a stronger bond with its customers, utilizes its existing customer base to extend its reach, and consistently pushes sales higher.

Cumulatively, these programs and others have helped Target create one of the strongest retail brands in the world and a store with an incredibly powerful reputation. This has also been felt on Wall Street where Dayton-Hudson continually has most-favored status with analysts. And because the chain is such a strong force in the retail industry, vendors go out of their way to develop special programs for them.

Target is a retailer by category, but the manner in which it conducts business has created a reputation that's unmatched by any other store.

While we've taken a closer look at Saturn and Target, if you think of companies that have powerful external reputations, you'll discover that the basics of what they do may not be that distinctive when compared to others in the same product or service classification, but "how they do it" sets them apart.

> Tiffany markets jewelry.
> Ben and Jerry's produces ice cream.
> Paul Newman creates salad dressings.
> FedEx delivers packages.
> Budweiser brews beer.
> Microsoft develops software.

NIKE makes athletic shoes.

All of the above are a part of basic product categories, yet every one of the companies mentioned above has a distinctly powerful reputation that's based on a series of actions. Your opinion of them is the result of cumulative actions that transcend the core competencies of what they do and have created memorable impressions because of "how" they do it.

Tiffany markets jewelry, but only Tiffany has jewelry designed by Elsa Pireti and Paloma Picasso with that signature blue box and white ribbon.

Ben and Jerry's produces ice cream, but they're the only ice cream maker that has flavors like Cherry Garcia and hold an annual meeting that's more like a Grateful Dead concert.

FedEx delivers packages, but they also deliver the assurance that "when it absolutely positively has to be there overnight," you can trust them to accomplish the task.

Budweiser brews beer, and in addition to more than four generations of brewing experience, they're the only brewing company that has a team of Clydesdales that tours the country and a team of "spokesfrogs."

NIKE makes athletic shoes, but no one else ever told us to "just do it" and inspired us with the likes of Michael Jordan and the best athletes in the world.

Think of any company you admire, and you'll undoubtedly be able to identify several attributes of "how" it does what it does that helps to create a distinctive perception and, ultimately, reputation with you and others.

The challenge of attracting the best and the brightest.

CREATING POWERFUL REPUTATION INTERNALLY

The challenge of attracting the best and the brightest.

Why worry about creating a powerful reputation internally? I mean, as long as customers buy the products and services you have to sell, what else matters?

Without employees to create, build, and service your product— you're out of business. It's that simple.

And gone are the days when running a classified ad or posting a sign in the window will generate many qualified applicants looking for work.

That may change if the current boom economy slows, and unemployment begins to edge up, but reality today means that businesses should be paying closer attention to their reputations among internal audiences. And even if the employment base expands and becomes more competitive, attracting and keeping the best and brightest will always remain a challenge.

The days of working for one organization for life are gone. Even if you show up, work hard, and contribute to the bottom line, you could still be gone tomorrow. Rightsizing, reengineering, mergers and acquisitions, and a near religious worship of shareholder value and return on investment means that everyone can be "replaced," or "given the opportunity to explore exciting new career dimensions."

Appropriately so, employee loyalty is a thing of the past as well. Talented individuals are finding organizations competing for their skills and the stakes are high: stock options, signing bonuses. When it comes to employee loyalty today, the operative phrase is "no guarantees."

"Candice Carpenter listened in shock as yet another of her ambitious young employees announced his resignation. Carpenter, 46, is chairwoman and CEO of iVillage, one of the Web's fastest growing online communities. Seven months earlier, she'd promoted this 26-year-old to an important job at the company, vice president of strategic development and operations, with an understanding that he would stay for at least a year. 'You made a commitment!' she said. He shrugged it off. ('We never had a contract,' he explained later.)"

(from "Stop The Fight," *Fast Company*, September 1998, 94.)

Instead, **the dialogue between companies and employees comes down to both asking each other, "What have you done for me lately?"**

While that may seem a bit cynical—and like anything, there are exceptions—but for the most part, business has evolved to an almost equal balance of power that requires employers and employees to live in an environment of tension that pushes both to produce.

If your company doesn't offer good benefits, competitive salaries, a piece of the profits—it won't keep or attract the best and the brightest. Even if it does, you better watch out because competitors have their eyes on your stars, and yesterday's bonus is no assurance of tomorrow's loyalty. As far as the employer is concerned, that was yesterday, and given the pace of business today, yesterday might as well be last year.

Conversely, for the employee, your idea that drove sales up last year was terrific. But what's the encore? How are you going to add value this year? What are your "deliverables" today?

Today, more than ever before, there is a balance of power between employers and employees. How long it will last is anyone's guess, but with low unemployment and high profitability, employers and employees are about as evenly matched as they've ever been.

Even so, there is a tension in the workplace. On the one hand, employers are asking employees to be more innovative. On a global level, the speed at which business moves today on a is unprecedented. Yesterday's innovation is readily knocked off, copied, and marked down in price.

On the other hand, pressure to assure return on investment remains high and efficiency in the name of profitability is prized. Do more with less and faster.

How employers and employees interact with each other in such an environment is critical to both groups. **Since employees spend more time on the job than ever before, with organizations providing a host of financial as well as social needs for people, internal communications take on a new importance.**

Want to limit your planned internal dialogue to a top-down monthly newsletter? Get real. Whatever you're publishing is old news, and if it's of any value, the information has more than likely been spread throughout the organization via e-mail and gossip-net within hours, if not minutes, of its occurring.

Your employees are your number one emissaries to the world. How they communicate with one another, with vendors, customers, and prospective employees is one of the greatest determinants in the reputation equation. Equally important is how you have discussions with them and disseminate information to them.

The method by which you interact with this group encompasses a broad array of tools.

Even though I previously cited a traditional means like a newsletter, you need to expand how you view conversations with internal audiences if you're concerned with reputation.

Benefits are a major tool in your ongoing dialogue with employees. As the lines between work and home continue to blur and meld, companies are becoming much more paternalistic. Basic health care is taken for granted; in fact, its mandated. Progressive organizations are taking this to the next level with expanded, innovative programs that take into account everything from benefits coverage for same sex partners to offering on-site daycare.

Do you have a program or set-aside time for employees to be creative and work on projects of personal interest? What about classes on safe driving that employees can take on their lunch hour and upon completion reduce their auto insurance rates, or giving them paid time off to participate in an organized exercise program (which benefits the employee through better health while reducing the use of the company health plan and the number of sick days taken)? How about a retreat center or recreation facility where employees can go either on their own or with their families?

How much is continuing education supported and how available is it to all employees, not just the folks in corner offices?

And speaking of offices, how innovative is the environment that's been created for employees? In one innovative example—a company in our organization called FAME—you step off the elevators and sixteen miniature video screens are overhead, all tuned to a different channel. Walk toward the reception desk, and you pass a set of heavy red stage drapes. On your left are wild theatre props, including some flying monkeys from a local production of *The Wizard of Oz*. On a brick wall to the right is genuine stage rigging, complete with ropes. In front of you is a thirty-foot mural of Michelangelo's *Creation*.

You can imagine what guests say when they get off the elevators—but imagine how employees feel when they walk into work everyday? Creative? Energized? More like going to play than to work?

FAME is all about creating innovative and stimulating environments and products for its clients, so it uses its own offices to create a setting that supports its work and speaks volumes to its employees every day about the kind of company it is.

Developing a keener sense of awareness about your organization and the multiple ways it converses with employees is probably the most valuable thing you can do in order to better understand and develop the progress to build your internal reputation. Review the following list, add to it if necessary, and note what you communicate to employees and how the message (if any) is delivered.

Health care

Retirement plans

Profit sharing

Competitive information

Mission statement

Flex time

Office environment

Salary surveys

Professional development

Insurance

Annual and quarterly earnings

Vacation policies

Parking

Recreation facilities

New hires/fires

Child care

Quality standards

Capital improvements

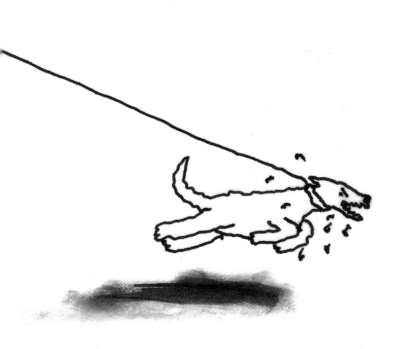

"You are what we say you are."
THE MEDIA

THE FOURTH ESTATE

"Remember, son, many a good story has been ruined by over-verification."

James Gordon Bennett

"He who can lick can bite."

French proverb

It now seems quite evident that what we do and how we do it determines who we are and what our reputation becomes. Yet another variable also can exert a powerful influence over the equation when and if it becomes part of the mix: how actions are interpreted or appraised by third-party information providers—the media. Look back to the original syllogism for reputation, and you see how important media appraisal becomes, especially when you take into account the incredible reach that publications, broadcast, and on-line media have:

**Manifestation of thought
or instinct creates action.
Action creates experience.
Experience creates the basis for appraisal.
Appraisal creates the basis for reputation.
(Therefore, action creates reputation.)**

In business or in our personal lives, what the media reports can have a dramatic impact on reputation and this can translate directly to the bottom line. **From identifying and perpetuating trends to**

interpreting actions, the media exerts a powerful influence over reputation. Individuals and organizations that understand how the media works can exercise greater influence over how their reputation is created and translated.

The media environment has changed dramatically in the last decade. Ten years ago major broadcast networks and daily newspapers ruled. Today the world of reputation-influencing media is as rich and complex as the number and variety of channels, Web sites, and publications available.

We live in a marketplace that has been transformed by something called the demassification of markets, which is basically the fragmentation of consumer segments in the population. Since media serves different segments of the population, shifts in the population create opportunities for new media vehicles. While providing an accurate gauge to tell us where the media is headed, these shifts also can tell us where we should be looking to create and influence reputation in the future.

And in the midst of all this change, there's a new form of media called the Internet that's rewriting all the rules of the game, creating equal amounts of chaos and opportunity in the reputation arena.

So, what do you do in this dynamic media environment if you're concerned about your organization's reputation? Take a lesson from the world of marketing and real estate—in these two disciplines the two guiding principles are: Focus and location.

When it comes to developing your reputation, media is brand reputation real estate and you want to be in the prime neighborhoods.

Media = Real Estate
Prime Media = Prime Neighborhoods = Better Reputation

Just like there are good and bad sides of the tracks when it comes to real estate, the same holds true for your reputation. Where your reputation resides in the media has a value for many different publics from employees to Wall Street analysts. **The value of companies will literally rise and fall on a regular basis depending on what is reported about them.** A multitude of other audiences also are impacted by this information. Just try to recruit talented employees or obtain favorable credit terms and financing if your organization is reported to be "troubled." These aren't the only audiences who will be wary, potential customers and vendors may think twice about becoming involved with a company that's having problems.

That's the dark side. The sun also can shine brightly, especially for organizations that garner favorable media coverage. **Companies and brands that win favorable coverage from the media literally cash in on something more powerful than any advertising can buy—the implied endorsement of what is perceived as an objective third-party.** And the better the neighborhood the endorser comes from, the more powerful the impact.

Before any advertising, Volkswagen's new Beetle had waiting lists of thousands of buyers who had read, seen, and heard media accounts about the new car.

No matter how clever and creative, a company's advertising is a paid endorsement from a subjective party. Everyone knows the space has been purchased to deliver a message that's been crafted to persuade and sell. That's not the case with media coverage.

Editorial coverage of a company or a brand is eminently more believable and influential than a sponsored message. Just ask yourself, which carries more weight and credibility—a favorable review of a product in a credible publication like *Consumer Report* or a one-time paid advertisement proclaiming the virtues of the product?

When it comes to service-driven brands, the same holds true. The legendary Nordstrom retail chain doesn't advertise the fact that it has a reputation for unparalleled service. Still, we know this is true because of the countless media stories over the years that have related situations such as customers returning snow tires for refunds, even though the retailer doesn't sell automotive supplies.

If the product happens to be a professional service, like accounting, reputation is just as important or perhaps even more important. Economists call the professional services category "credence goods," meaning goods that are purchased primarily on the basis of reputation.

Now, I'm not proposing that marketers abandon their advertising programs or diminish the importance of that communications strategy, because while media relations is a powerful tool, it's rare that you can attain and sustain levels of frequency alone that can carry the day. For instance you can't always rely on the media to point out all of the important features and advantages of your product or service. However, when integrated with advertising and other paid marketing communication, media relations can be a very strategic tool. Of all the marketing communications variables, it probably has the most powerful influence on reputation.

If you want to utilize media relations as a tool to influence reputation, you need to understand it better than an advertising media planner with $100 million to spend. Beyond assessing rating points and station rankings, you need to have a strong grasp of how the media works. **Understanding how content is created is paramount to developing and executing a strong media relations program in the context of an overall reputation creation plan.** Once you know this, you have a strategic tool for creating and shaping reputation. Misunderstand or abuse your relationship with the media, and you run the risk of damaging reputation and credibility.

For starters, the media is not the enemy. Contrary to what you may have heard or read about tabloid sensationalism, trashy talk shows, and "investigative" reporters playing fast and lose with the facts during rating periods, the legitimate press is, for the most part, reasonable and objective. Still, this knowledge doesn't wipe out the image of Mike Wallace of 60 Minutes putting someone on the hot seat on national television. However, unless your organization engages in something controversial or has something to hide, you'll never have to worry about Mike Wallace showing up at your door.

Even though the media is not "the enemy," like any other business, it has customers that it needs to retain and grow market share in order to remain in business. Since the media derives most of its revenue from advertising sales, the readership, viewership, and listener numbers are important. When shaping content, media outlets on one hand must take into account the needs and wants of the media consuming public while still keeping an eye toward maintaining and attracting new consumers. Balancing these needs and wants of the public with journalistic standards is a fine line they must walk every day. But don't rely on them to tell your story or to get it right, if they do. In today's time-compressed, competitive media culture, you have to tell your own story. Some call it putting "spin" on your own point of view.

Forget what you read and hear about spin. The media regard spin as public relations manipulation, but spin is nothing more than your side of the story. In some instances, someone tries to put a favorable spin on their point of view, and sometimes the boundaries of truth get stretched or outright violated by unethical communications people, organizations, and journalists as well. But given the fact that the world we live in today is one of instantaneous communication where everyone can have their own media base (called a Web site on the Internet), your point of view or spin is a way of life. If you don't represent yourself or your organization's point of view, who will?

The state of journalism today is seemingly more sensationalistic than it's ever been. Combine this with the general public's insatiable daily need for content and the only way you can be certain your point of view is appropriately represented is by being proactive.

Call it spin, or whatever you like, but ask yourself this: who is best qualified to interpret your actions—you or a stranger? Who would you prefer to interpret your actions?

Think for a second about your own media habits. The world we live in is a complex web of political, economic, and sociologic relationships. We turn to the media for insight and interpretation. Merely reporting the basics of who, what, where, when, why, and how no longer meets our need for understanding. As complexity increases, so does the need for deeper explanation, and the media serves an invaluable role as distiller and interpreter. Also, while we want deeper understanding and interpretation of our increasingly complex world, we want it in shorter more manageable "bites," in full color, and if there is some type of an entertainment component to it as well, all the better.

At the same time, we are asking more from the media, the media has become leaner (and, in some cases, meaner). Faced with recent trends in downsizing, the media, like most corporations today, has had to do more with less. In other words, it's had to be marketplace-driven and do what it could to increase circulation and viewership in the face of new media threats, while still upholding journalistic standards. It's a difficult position to be in, but luckily the media doesn't have to do it all alone.

Understanding the position of the media enables you to effectively work with them and to help them do their job better. Remember, the media needs content on a daily basis, and if you can help in the process known as "feeding the beast," you can not only play a role in shaping your organization's reputation, you also provide a service to the media.

Understand first that media is about space.

Column inches, airtime, outdoor signage, Internet sites—it's all about space. Again using our real estate analogy, the media is a broker of space. Space is its inventory and you can either buy it (advertising) or lease a portion (media relations). Buy an ad and you're purchasing a piece of media real estate where you can pretty much do whatever you want. Utilize media relations and you get a short-term lease, only this time it comes with an influential roommate that gets to not only make the rules, but also have the final say (although there may be some a little room for negotiation).

Today, there's an incredible amount of space for sale and lease. Buying is no problem as long as you can afford the price. Leasing is more complicated with constantly changing terms and requirements. If you want to lease, know the terms of your landlords and roommates—know what the media wants and needs. What they want and need is the content their consumers want. Content is the substance that creates readers, viewers, and listeners, and the quantity and quality of this population determines the desirability and subsequent price of media real estate for buyers (advertisers).

Given the competition among media today, the content that's created must also be compelling enough to attract readers, viewers, and listeners. What makes a story compelling in journalism is no different than in the theatre, and that's drama and conflict. Good versus evil, David versus Goliath. Real life conflict creates interest and interest translates to readers, viewers, and listeners. In some cases, a one-quarter dip in earnings can become "the beginning of the end of a successful profit run." An unexplained inquiry from a government regulatory agency becomes "potentially serious regulatory action in the works" in the hands of an over zealous or inexperienced reporter.

In fact, a friend of mine who works as a reporter for one of the largest newspaper chains in the country confided in me that at a recent in-house seminar they were told to find the conflict or opposing point of view in every story, no matter what, not for balanced viewpoints, but because readers "want" conflict. So, if twenty economists are bullish about the future, find one that's a bear. If a dozen environmental groups applaud the efforts of a company to control emissions, find one that sees eminent danger. A good story has drama with a beginning, middle, and end that either leads to conflict resolution or sets the stage for continuing chapters.

"The first essence of journalism
is to know what you want to know;
the second, is to find out who will tell you."
—John Gunther

Given such a playing field and the variables involved, you may be wondering—why take the risk at all? A financial client of mine lives by the rule that the whale only gets harpooned when it rises to the surface and can be seen—so some would say be safe and stay beneath the media radar. While that adage may have been true when it originated decades ago, no whale today can stay beneath the surface undetected anymore (besides, whales have to breathe sometime). **And as long as you and your organization operate responsibly and ethically, there's far more reputation equity to gain than to lose when it comes to media coverage of your company and brand (and if you don't operate according to standards, the media can play an important role in explaining your position to your many publics).**

Every year, the most successful companies in the country support their brands by utilizing media relations to create millions of dollars of "free" media coverage. They create a dialogue with various publics that have greater credibility than a one-way paid-for communication like advertising.

"What kills a skunk is the publicity
it gives itself."
—Abraham Lincoln

FOCUS AND LOCATION APPLIED
TO MEDIA RELATIONS

The first rule of marketing is knowing what business you're in, and what your company is all about. In "Marketing Myopia," *Harvard Business Reviews* examined a classic example of one industry that missed the boat, or in this instance, the plane. During the infancy of the passenger airline industry, the railroads made a serious strategic error by thinking they were in the railroad business rather than understanding they were in the transportation business. Meanwhile, they watched as the airlines chipped away at their customer base. The lesson is—know what your business is about.

While this may seem like an obvious step and something we take for granted, knowing what our business stands for goes well beyond the lofty mission statement, although that's often a good place to start. **Mission statements and brand promises should be aspirational and reflect where the organization wants to go or how it wants to be perceived in the future. Know that and you have a clear picture of not only where you want your organization's reputation to go but also where you want to focus your reputation building media relations efforts.**

Go back to our list of key audiences, and list the aspirational positions you want your organization to occupy within each group. Here's an example of what your grid may look like. If you're a company with a strong customer service focus:

Audience	Aspirational Position
Customers	Unique, distinctive, service-oriented company:
	• no haggle selling
	• strong guarantee program
	• supportive customer service "legend" stories
	• enthusiastic employees committed to quality

For every audience base and position, you need to identify supporting points of compelling fact that you can build a story around (a compelling fact is one that has significant meaning to both parties in the relationship). This process may be time consuming, but once you clearly articulate the reputation you want to have with a particular audience and identify the supporting variables and specific examples of those variables that provide evidence of your aspirational position, your media relations strategy begins to take shape.

Take a look at the Saturn organization. Saturn is all about creating something new in the automotive industry—an organization that focuses on a process and is based on what consumers and employees want. When introduced, it was a totally new way to run a car company.

As Saturn set about building its reputation franchise with customers through media relations, oddly enough, it did everything but focus on the car itself. Rarely did you read a story about how fast a Saturn could go from 0 to 60 in a quarter-mile. Instead you saw stories that talked about how you can buy a car without haggling when it came down to price. You saw how Saturn consultants were there to provide service, not to try to see how high a price they could get for a vehicle. You saw how an Ivy League graduate was so impressed with the process, he became a Saturn consultant.

Saturn understood exactly what reputation position it wanted to occupy with consumers, and then looked at every variable that would support that position and developed media relations strategies for each.

Once you know the reputation position you want to occupy with a specific audience and identify the supporting, compelling facts that provide evidence of your claims, you need to identify the best media vehicles for delivering the story to the audience.

LOCATION

Using the real estate analogy introduced earlier, I want to identify the best neighborhoods for reputation to lease space.

Look at the vehicles in which your organization advertises or places it would advertise if it had the budget. Where do your targets live—literally and figuratively? **In order to reach your audience, you have to know where they are. You also have to know who they are and what their media habits are.**

One example of how to do it comes from the health care division of 3M. Just this past year my agency worked with 3M to introduce a new bandage with colorful designs for kids. Considering that there were two influencing targets (children and parents), but one primary purchaser (parents), we sought to reach parents and kids alike. To reach parents we targeted parenting magazines, other publications that have parenting columns, and daily newspaper columns that address new products for children. For the younger key influencer, kids, we targeted media specific publications and programming. In this case, our product garnered editorial placements in publications like *Sports Illustrated For Kids* and *Teen* magazine.

While a media placement in *Popular Mechanics* would have done wonders to boost the total number of consumer impressions generated, the exposure wouldn't have helped very much in reaching the target audiences for the product.

You may also want to consider the season in which you launch your product and, if appropriate, find a tie-in. In this case, the colorful bandage was launched in late spring, just in time for the "cuts and scrapes season," which we brought to viewer's attention at more than 100 television stations as part of their seasonal programming news segments.

Creating a grid of media outlets gets more complicated with the thousands of variables that exist. You may need help in putting it together, but once you have your map you can begin to know the territory. **Knowing the territory means knowing what the media wants. To know what they want, you not only have to know them, you also have to ask them.**

Start by becoming a student of their publications, stations, and programs. Nothing irritates a member of the press more than someone who contacts them with a request and knows nothing about the content of their particular media vehicle.

Know the media vehicle first and, if possible, something about the reporter, or at least the format and tone of the section in which you want to appear. With that knowledge, you can develop your strategy for asking to lease some reputational real estate.

Bottom line when it comes to media relations
for building reputation? Don't wait.
Be proactive. The companies you read about
more than likely have an aggressive media
relations program in place. Why do you think
you're reading about them? They know who their
customers are and what their media habits are.
They're cultivating relationships with the media
not by harassing them with pointless news
releases and bothersome telephone calls,
but by understanding what they need and then
providing them with content that
meets that need.

*Are you giving your reputation
the attention it deserves?*

THE CARE PRINCIPLE

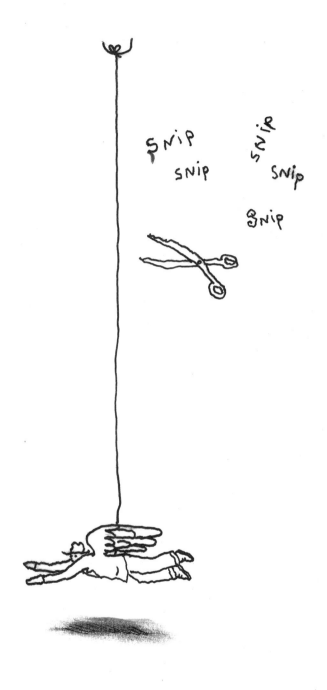

Conscious
Acts of
Reputation
Everyday

Reputations can be created or destroyed in a given moment by a single act. However, for the vast majority of organizations, reputations are created over time through cumulative actions taken day after day, month after month, year after year. And while no company consciously sets out to destroy its reputation, by not consciously creating and nurturing the relationships it has with key publics, reputations can erode over time or be overshadowed by competitors that aggressively seek to build more powerful relationships.

Nordstrom didn't acquire a reputation for outstanding customer service through a single act. 3M isn't regarded as one of the leading organizations in the world when it comes to innovation because of an isolated incident or product. For both of these organizations and scores of others that enjoy positive, powerful reputations, their reputations have been earned and reinforced by consistent, cumulative actions.

The same applies to individuals as well. For instance, Frank Lloyd Wright is revered in architecture because of the cumulative body of work he created in his career. The same applies to individuals in every discipline you can think of, and it applies to you as well.

Remembering that action creates experience which forms the basis for appraisal, our actions over time create the reputation we have as individuals and as organizations.

You create something by taking action. By striking one of the keys on my laptop computer, I've created something. This action moves me closer to a desired end result, such as completing a manuscript. This in turn helps to further my reputation with my editor as someone who meets his deadlines. However, not everything we do moves us toward creating more powerful reputations.

If you're like most of the people in the world, a majority of your time is spent unconsciously creating. In other words, most of your daily actions are habitual and instinctual, usually focused on short-term goals. While there's nothing wrong with that, if we want to create a more powerful reputation, we also need times when we move from unconscious creating to conscious creating.

Unfortunately in the business world, most conscious creating gets reserved for annual planning and corporate retreats, and even then the concept of creating reputation is seldom, if ever, discussed. **Reputation is an assumed outcome of marketing, and ultimately, profitability.** It's a direct result of your market positioning. It's your advertising. It's what PR does. When considered, if ever, it's usually viewed as an outcome of other action plans that more than likely were not created with a reputational objective or goal.

"Many are called but few get up."
—Oliver Herford

To some extent, the current obsession with brand is a concern about reputation. After all, a brand is simply something that has identity. And most of the pontificating about brand is focused on one end result—selling to someone. In that respect, most brand discussion falls short because it doesn't take into consideration the other variables that must be in place in order to create a desired brand perception.

In order for a brand promise to be kept, it requires the efforts of everyone involved in an organization. In essence, we must consciously create those actions that are consistent with and support the desired reputation we want our brand to have.

The reputation of a brand, which is its most valuable asset and the basis for all further brand development, is a dependent variable that is created by the cumulative actions of thousands of independent variables that occur every day among multiple audiences.

A brand promise is nothing more than an aspirational statement that, if kept, will create a desired reputation for our product or service among the audiences with whom we seek to create relationships. However, unless the multiple audiences that create action, and thus reputation, every day on behalf of our product or service consciously create these actions with the brand promise in mind, we run the risk of not keeping the stated promise and even worse, creating inconsistency in reputation.

We are all brands to some extent, and when we work with others toward a common goal, say in a department within an organization, we become part of a larger organizational brand. The

ultimate product or service brand that is sold is actually the cumulative result of the hundreds, thousands, even millions of individual and group brands in a given organization. Looking back to Olins's formula of corporate identity, a simple syllogism drives the creation of reputation and the ultimate success for a brand, whether it is our personal brand or a global product.

What we want to be (our desired reputation)
IS DEPENDENT ON

What we choose to do
+ <u>How we choose to do it</u>
What we will become

So, the questions to be asking are relatively simple, but the process becomes more complex when applied across multiple audiences. What do we want our reputation to be with employees, customers, vendors, regulators, and everybody these audiences come in contact with? **While our reputation may not be precisely the same for every audience, common and unifying elements that cross and intersect through every public can create powerful reputation. In the end, it's the cumulative actions across all these groups and others involved in your organization that will determine what your reputation becomes—and these actions can be conscious, everyday acts.**

When you're creating reputation, the product you're creating is the organization. Your organizational "product" is comprised of multiple brand images: marketing, human resources, research and development, vendor relations, media and community relations, investor and financial relations. In order to create consistent, powerful reputation, everyone needs to understand that their specific brand discipline contributes to and creates the organizational reputation.

In order to imbue the spirit and commitment of conscious creation on a personal and organizational level, those involved must understand that reputations are created over time beginning with a single action that generates an experience that is subsequently appraised. From that point on, you or your organization begin to move on a reputation continuum.

This is where research can really pay off. It helps you find where you are on the continuum. Organizations spend millions of dollars annually talking to those individuals whose appraisals they deem important. They take surveys and conduct focus groups with consumers, employees, and analysts to determine where they are on someone's relationship continuum, or where they might be if they created something new. Research is a snapshot of a product's or company's relationship continuum, which is valuable information to a point, but this "snapshot" is also one of the problems with research. It's merely a still frame in the fast-forward movie of business.

Where you are today is not necessarily where you might be tomorrow, which it why its important to continually track where you are. Even more important than tracking, however, is to be continually and consciously creating and cultivating reputation.

Organizations realizing the limitations of research have started relying on trend forecasting. A person in this occupation, a "futur-ist," is paid for telling organizations what kind of world their cus-tomers are going to be living in and what the implications of that will be for their relationship with that customer. However, this fore-casting is primarily done in regard to product development.

If you want to create truly powerful reputation across all the brands you have, you're going to need to be a reputation futurist and project what is the most powerful reputational position you should occupy based on where the business environment is going to be in the future. And remember, it's not just about consumer and business-to-business products—it's about the future of your reputation across your employee relations brand, customer service brand, vendor relations brand, banking relationships brand, and media relations brand.

In order to move toward a desired reputation in the future, you need to be aware of your actions every day. How they move you toward that goal, and what every individual in an organization can do to consciously create those actions that will cumulatively have the effect of moving the organization forward on its reputation con-tinuum.

Starting on an individual level and branching upwards to depart-ment and divisional levels, desired reputational objectives and strategies should be set against all audiences. Just as individual and departmental performance goals are set, everyone in an organiza-tion can be working toward reputation goals that support a variety of brands throughout the business.

Moving forward, to develop reputation objectives and strategies, some form of audit should occur in order to identify an individual's or organization's current position and where movement needs to occur in order to develop and optimize reputation to reach a desired end.

While the methodology for gathering data may vary by the resources available, anyone can find out what their individual or organizational reputation is by identifying key audience segments and gathering information in a few key areas.

For individuals, asking supervisors and peers can be an effective way to determine reputation. Many leadership training courses utilize confidential questionnaires to an individual's direct reports, peers, and supervisors to determine strengths and weaknesses.

For departments, divisions, and organizations as a whole, the process is similar, however, the audiences differ.

In each case, you want to identify the elements that are important to a given audience as they determine your reputation. For example, service support may rank high on the list for the customers of a manufacturing organization, while garnering favorable product reviews by consumer publications may top the list for a high ticket hard-goods marketer. For a high-flying Silicon Valley software start-up, the ability to offer stock options to gifted potential employees may be a primary determinant of employee relations success, and to an innovative medical products company, winning regulatory approval is a must for business to occur at all.

There's no standard ranking of audience priorities, and every organization's goals will vary, but unless you have an idea of what's important to a given segment, you won't be able to efficiently and effectively move your reputation on its continuum.

Once you identify and rank your audience segments, there are some basic areas in which to probe:

Rank the order of reputation variables to segment. (How important are the variables in relation to each other?)

Overall perceived competence? (What grade do you give yourself on each variable?)

Competence in comparison to competitors? (Your grades compared to the grades of your competitors?)

Perceived strengths?
Perceived strengths versus competitors?
(What do you do better or worse than your competition?)

Perceived weaknesses?
Perceived weaknesses versus competitors?
(Where are you vulnerable versus your competitors?)

Specific areas for improvement in relation to rank ordered reputation variables?
(Target areas for improvement based on reputation priorities?)

Blocks and barriers to improvement?
(What will prevent you from improving on the target areas identified above?)

Specific identification of success points or overall measurement of success?
(How will you gauge success, and at what regular intervals will you measure?)

CHAPTER TEN

In essence, you want to find out what the most important determinants of reputation are within the audience segments that impact your business, and then determine what you can do to strengthen your reputational position to those segments.

*Or, in other words,
no matter where you go, there you are.*

YOU ARE WHO YOU ARE

*Or, in other words,
no matter where you go, there you are.*

In the age of reputation, the smart individual applies the same reputation creation principles to their own career that they would to their organization. Just like companies, individuals acquire a reputation that is a significant, if not the most significant, factor in their ability to succeed, not just in business, but on a personal level as well.

Common sense, right? Yes. Yet how many of us consciously evaluate and establish goals for what we want our reputation to be? So many of us create programs for our companies, products, and clients, yet we leave little time to create the most important reputation of all—our own.

You're beginning to see more being published in cyberspace and in the physical space of books and periodicals about things like "being your own brand." The popular, new business monthly, *Fast Company,* even devoted a whole section to this topic and created a web site about being your own brand. But you know what? **Thinking of yourself as a brand is old news for people who understand that what it really comes down to in the end is reputation.**

What perceptions do you have when you read the following names?

Michael Jordan

George Washington

Oprah Winfrey

Lee Iacocca

Neil Simon

Georgia O'Keefe

As far as I'm concerned, you are what my perception of you says you are—until I have reason to believe differently. You are whatever your reputation is—good or bad—until proven otherwise by a jury of your peers.

So, ask yourself this: **What have you done for your reputation lately?**

As a starting point, you should find out what your reputation is among the audiences that count most to you. This doesn't have to be a terribly sophisticated research project. In fact, here's a very simple way that it can be done, almost like a performance review.

1. Make a list of professional and personal contacts whose opinions matter most to you.

2. Draft a cover letter that explains that you're undertaking a reputation audit of yourself because you want to: have a more positive impact on the world around you; embark on a self-improvement program; want to identify your strengths and work on your weaknesses—whatever reasons you feel comfortable sharing.

3. Explain that the responses will be confidential and enclose a postage-paid envelope that's addressed to a friend that will collect the responses and forward them to you.

4. Have them address three basic questions:

a) What do you perceive to be my reputation? Please draft a statement and be as specific as possible.

b) What specific strengths do I possess that enhance my

reputation?

c) Are there ways that I could further strengthen my reputation in the context in which you know me?

Armed with some solid feedback, you are ready to apply the same principles from the last chapter and begin creating your own powerful reputation. If you focus on the variables you identify from your personal reputation audit and apply "conscious acts of reputation everyday," you'll begin to shape the way others perceive you. By modifying the "probe" questions from the last chapter, you can utilize the data from your personal reputation audit to develop an action plan.

1. Rank order your reputation variables in importance to you.

2. Assess what your strengths and weaknesses are.

3. Identify the areas that need more immediate attention or are problematic to you.

4. Rank all areas for improvement in order of importance to you.

5. Identify the blocks and barriers that may prevent you from making the changes you want to make—and identify what you can do to overcome them.

6. Put together your CARE plan and identify elements you can measure along the way to determine your progress (quarterly at a minimum).

7. Plan to re-audit your opinion leaders to determine external reputation progress.

It won't happen overnight, but if you make a conscious effort to enhance your reputation by setting weekly, monthly, quarterly, and annual goals in relation to both your career and personal life, you'll begin to affect change.

The key is to start with a long range plan. For your career, set two reputation goals that you can work on for a twelve month period. If you want to take on more, you can always add to the list. Once you've identified two or more, break your goals down into specific objectives, strategies, and tactics—just like an effective business plan.

Next, write a positioning statement that encompasses the areas of reputation you want to create. If you'd like, use the one below and begin with your name and your company or department name if appropriate:

(name of person or organization)

_____

is known and respected for his/her/its abilities to

_____

_____

_____

_____

because he/she/it consistently

_____

_____

_____

and the value of that is

_____

_____

_____.

What you're doing is basically identifying your reputation objectives and then the strategies and behaviors that will support the objectives. These are then reinforced by a value statement or benefit.

In addition to treating your reputation as a measurable variable that you can plan to influence, keep in mind some overall guidelines as you set about creating a course of action.

There is something to thinking in a brand context about reputation. Carl Speak, a brand consultant who helps *Fortune* 500 companies develop brands and helps their marketing personnel better understand those brands and how to make them stronger, believes that great brands are aspirational. Great reputations are aspirational as well. Great reputations don't rest on their laurels—they consistently look for new challenges. Develop new aspirational reputation goals once you achieve the ones you previously set.

Bear in mind an advertising idea championed years ago by legendary adman Rosser Reeves: have a Unique Selling Proposition (USP). According to Reeves, every product should have a unique proposition. Likewise, your reputation, your product, should have a unique offering. It was also Reeves' idea that this unique proposition should be hammered into consumer consciousness through irritatingly high levels of frequency, and in time, the USP concept was abandoned. Wisk's "ring around the collar, ring around the collar," is a great example. However, modify Reeves' concept (sans the frequency levels) and you get: **create your own Unique Reputation Proposition, or in other words, find ways you can define yourself and stand out.**

Remember that the same principles of reputation that apply to organizations also apply to you. What you do and how you do it will determine what your reputation is, and what you choose to do in the future and how you choose to do it will determine what your reputation will be in the future.

We're all like professional service consultants, like lawyers and accountants, who deal in credence goods or goods purchased based on reputation. The things you do on a daily basis establish the desirability of the credence goods you have to market. So, what can you market to someone or get someone interested in on the basis of your reputation (the answer could be yourself or your ideas)? What is the value of your credence goods, the ones that people will buy based on the good faith of your reputation?

For some additional help, think of people and brands whose reputations you admire. Then, find out as much as you can about them. How do they do what they do? Read their biographies. Get on line and learn everything you can about a company. Get a copy of their annual report. **Find the essence of what makes the brands and the people you admire great—it usually comes down to a few basic things. Innovation. Integrity. Diligence. Honesty. Commitment. Service.** It doesn't have to be complicated, and with great companies it seldom is. In fact, it's usually so simple that every employee and every vendor and every customer can easily understand the essence of what a company or individual is about. And when it comes right down to it, this is what you will find at the core of their reputation.

Here's a creative exercise to get you started in building your reputation, or creating your very own brand. It's one that toy inventor, Charlie Girsch, and I use in a graduate course we teach together on the creative process.

Create a logo for yourself.

We ask the individuals in our class to create a logo for themselves and then everyone in the class lines up and has thirty seconds to explain it to one of their classmates. By the time everyone has explained their logo to twenty or so people, they've been able to narrow the focus and get to the core of what their logo, and they themselves, are all about.

So, get out a pad and some crayons, or get on a Mac. Cut and paste, make a collage. Create something that's a little more of a stretch than where you may see yourself today (remember, aspirational) and keep it around to remind you to CARE about your reputation.

The logo for my own company, Karwoski & Courage, is a lion that's roaring. The lion is a visual symbol of my partner, "courage," since there is no individual named courage in the agency. Rather, the name comes from the Latin word *coer*, which means heart or essence. The earliest translation of the word was to the French *corage*, which meant heart, mind, and spirit. All of those qualities embodied what I wanted the agency to bring to our clients every day, and the lion on our logo is a visual reminder to me of the reputation I want myself and the agency to have.

YOU ARE WHO YOU ARE

Time to dust off your crystal ball.

FUTURE REPUTATION

Time to dust off your crystal ball.

Planning for what you want your reputation to be takes hard work and a crystal ball. It's hard work to identify the significant trends that will affect not only society but also the work/industry environment of the future. The crystal ball helps interpret how these trends can and will impact your world and that of your organization in the years to come.

Unless you play futurist and forecaster to some extent, you won't be able to craft and manage your reputation. It may seem a lofty goal to think that we can change global, societal, and business forces, however, by anticipating change and understanding the environment, we can move proactively to create a desired reputation.

The difference is proactive creation based on a vision that occurs within the context of environmental understanding rather than consequential results that occur from a reactionary position.

You can create what you want to be based on your vision and desire and a projection of what the environment for creation will be, or you can wait and respond to whatever happens to you. Proactive versus reactive.

So, what's on the agenda according to the societal crystal ball? Connections. Speed. Control.

CONNECTIONS

The society of speed is being brought to you now, and will be arriving even faster to you tomorrow, by your omnipresent friend, technology. I give you more connections than you're capable of handling: the facsimile machine, electronic voice messaging, electronic mail, satellite messaging systems, cellular satellite telephony, the World Wide Web, and more to come.

We have in our power the ability to communicate with virtually anyone in the world almost instantaneously. The implications are and continue to be staggering in every aspect of life, especially in business. In business, markets that never existed before have opened.

The phenomenon of "virtual" businesses create competition where it's never existed in the past.

Production and distribution processes and the traditional channels of sales and marketing have changed dramatically. **Like it or not, we offer our reputation to a world that is infinitely connected and interconnected.**

Because technology enables us to transmit information about reputation with incredible speed, a bad product review can be posted on an Internet site in New York and minutes later be accessed and acted upon in Bangkok.

In this environment and as we become even more connected, with greater convenience at greater speed, reputations will be created and evaluated on a continual basis by an ever-increasing number of people. The upside potential is incredible for those individuals and companies with powerful reputations, just as the downside is for those evaluated unfavorably or with marginal reputations.

Our connectedness will provide two options and implications for reputation. The first is that more informal evaluative networks will be (and are being) created. While there have always been informal and formal affinity groups for various topics and activities, the Internet exponentially expands our ability to connect and interact. The evolution of chat groups and user groups relating to virtually any subject means that our reputation can be scrutinized in a very segmented manner among the most critical of audiences.

The converse of all this connectivity is the overwhelming nature of it all. Given ever increasing speed, the time we have to connect is still limited. So, while there may be scores of chat groups and user Web sites, we'll prioritize accordingly. That means that a new order of influencers will evolve in our industries and specialty domains. As we continue to connect, new priority groups and individuals will inevitably emerge and be added to continually reshuffled lists of those we must consider when creating our reputation.

Right now we're seeing an emerging discipline called knowledge management. Knowledge management is, at its essence, about maximizing the efficient utilization of the tons of data made available through all this wonderful connectivity.

Knowledge management basically asks the question, "What do we do with all this information, and is there some way we can use it (analyze it, cross tabulate it, share it) to do things better?" And one of the variables that will be examined, either directly or indirectly, through an analysis of different performance factors in the knowledge management process is overall reputation. In fact, evaluating reputation may become the ultimate (although probably initially unconscious) outcome of the knowledge management process.

SPEED

"Almost instantaneous communication and computation, for example, are shrinking time and focusing us on Speed. Connectivity is putting everybody and everything online in one way or another and has led to "the death of distance," a shrinking of space. Intangible value of all kinds, like service and information, is growing explosively, reducing the importance of tangible mass."

(from *"Blur, The Speed of Change in the Connected Economy,"* davis, meyer, 1989.)

Speed is where it's at.
Doing more in less time.
Drive down the cost of production and cost of service. Increase productivity.

The future game is to find out how fast you can go before you crash or burn up and out.

You've probably noticed that the pace of life and business has increased, or maybe you've been too busy to notice. Technology enables us to do more than ever before in less time, so we do more. If we could accomplish Task A in thirty minutes ten years ago and today we can accomplish Task A in five minutes, that means we add tasks to fill those extra twenty-five minutes—say Tasks B, C, and D—or at least that's what downsizing, rightsizing, reengineering, and productivity consultants would have us believe.

There's no doubt that we're able to do more, but the question becomes, "how much more can we do before it's too much?" How many tasks can we process? No one really knows, but the pace will continue to increase until some casualties begin to occur, just like the speed of an automobile or a plane, we'll keep testing limits.

So, what does speed mean for reputation?

It means that you and your organization better put on your digital running shoes and get in shape. You better be able to keep up, or you'll be passed up.

Unless you can move at the speed of business and society, your reputation will suffer.

Imagine someone in business today that doesn't have e-mail or voice mail. Do you even know of anyone that doesn't have these basic technologies?

When it comes to speed, it's not just the operational-excellence, value-discipline organizations that need to be on the cutting (bleeding) edge. By utilizing technology, companies as diverse as durable goods manufacturers and professional service providers can capitalize on making their offerings more efficient. That's the real advantage that speed provides.

You're going to have to move faster in the future and keep pace with your competitors. But the real key to utilizing speed to help build your reputation is harnessing the tools and the energy to work smarter, not necessarily harder.

When it comes to reputation, people and organizations want to partner with those individuals and companies that can either keep pace with them or set a pace for them to follow. As we move faster, activities become compressed and leave little time for mistakes. Those of us that can move swiftly and accurately will enjoy better reputations than those who fall behind, or fail to meet expectations because of trying to move too fast.

A caveat—make certain you pay special attention to internal audiences as your pace increases. The laws of physics apply here, and for every action there is definitely an equal and opposite reaction. Society is reacting to the ever-quickening pace by making an effort to consciously slow down. Homeostasis. That's why we're now seeing more and more self-help genre books on slowing down and finding simplicity. Business needs to keep pace, but not at any and all costs. Monitor your organization's reputation with internal audiences to ensure that your speed is under control, and make certain that your pace allows external audiences to have an opportunity to see who you are.

CONTROL

As we're speeding along and making more connections, some of us are already putting on the brakes in a desire for more control.

We're beginning to see a backlash of sorts to the ever-quickening pace and interconnectivity of personal and business life today. And while it's impressive to go faster and faster and become more and more connected, sooner or later it's going to be too much to manage. We're already in the midst of a slow down, simplification movement that's more than just a fad.

Just as the body regulates itself through the process of homeostasis, society and business reflect the same. If you imagine a rubber-band expanding and contracting, you have a pretty good picture of what's occurring right now.

Technology combined with a restoking of America's competitive fires has stretched the band to the point of breaking for many people, and the reaction is a desire to relieve the tension of the band. Hence, guides for simplicity and meditations for people who do too much. The desire for control.

Underlying the desire for control is a direct correlation to reputation that's tied to the two variables driving the desire—speed and connectivity.

Faster speeds combined with more connectivity and tasks places a premium on time. The greater the number of activities, the more we have a need for assurance and partners we know can keep up with us and help us to go faster. So, where do we look? To reputation.

The more potential connections, the more potential opportunities IF we partner with the right people and organizations. How will we decide, in this world filled with potential on the people and organizations that are right for us? Reputation.

We're seeing somewhat of a backlash to the "continually connected" state of being already. **Now, if you really want to impress people, you don't walk around looking like a cellular gunslinger with beepers and phones strapped to your sides. You're really cool if you can choose not to be in touch—it says that you're in control.** There's another movement that we're seeing that's related to the "choose not to be in touch," and that's the whole movement to simplify. Simplification is no fad, it's a bonafide trend that's becoming a way of life for many. **Simplification is a way of taking control.**

The way we live and the way we do business is like a pendulum. It swings to the extreme in one direction, comes back the other way in response, but eventually settles in the middle. That's what's happening now. Control is on one end of the pendulum's swing, and speed is on the other end.

The pace of life and business in general has become so fast, and we're so in touch that it's beginning to rub some people raw. Throw into that mix the last five years of corporate downsizing, and you begin to understand why people are beginning to take off their running shoes, slow down, and move toward more simplicity in their lives.

This whole phenomena is a bonanza for great brands and marketers because either way, they win. If things are moving too fast, you don't have time to make mistakes, so you buy the brands you trust the most. You go on reputation.

If you're trying to simplify and make things less complicated, there again it makes sense to buy based on reputation. After all, why complicate things by buying something that might not work. You're trying to reduce stress, not increase it.

So, what does the future of connectivity, speed and control mean for reputation? It means that reputation will increase in importance because every one of these variables serves to heighten reputation as a key consideration in any decision making process. It means that the consequences of strong and weak reputation will be more impactful. It means that reputation will ultimately play an even greater role in determining success and failure.

It means that companies and individuals that proactively create powerful reputations will create powerful futures for themselves.

THE END